The greatest wisdom is usually
associated with the fewest words.

SOPHOCLES

NO COPYRIGHT !

NO RIGHTS RESERVED

This book intentionally has no copyright. Any part of it may be shared freely, photographed, copied, faxed (?!), telegraphed, scanned, reproduced in any form or made into paper airplanes. Once you've read it, scribbled in the columns, tweeted your favourite quotes and Instagramed the pages, please pass it on to one of your friends. It should go without saying that whilst I'm happy for any part of this book to be freely shared, a credit would be nice.

To emphasise the point that anyone can (and should) write a book, I have written, edited, designed and formatted this entire book myself. I created the whole thing in 100 days and posted a photo of the progress each day on Instagram @JeremyWaite from 22nd March 2017. Since I have taken this approach to writing and publishing Ten Words, I must point out that **all the opinions, thoughts and comments expressed in this book are purely my own, and do not in any way represent that of my employer.** I am not trying to champion any particular brand or cause and I have accepted no money or incentives from any of the brands that feature in this book. This approach, I hope, will inspire others to write books of their own, but will also allow you the reader to forgive me any shortcomings in my grammar or the quality of my writing!

Regarding the people and brands that I have chosen to write about, I have tried to be fair and respectful at all times ~ and have carefully verified any facts, figures and statistics I have used. If any person, marketing team or brand owner feels that I have been in any way unfair, or infringed in any way (in full or in part) any of their intellectual property (including logo usage) please email me **JeremyWaite@Me.com** and I will be happy to rectify any amendments or inaccuracies immediately, and correct them for any further printings. Thanks for reading this small, but important print.

Cover design image courtesy of Shutterstock.
Designed on a Mac using Adobe Creative Cloud and Microsoft Office 365.
Typeset in American Typewriter, Urania Czech and Calibri.
Printed in the United States by Lulu.com, Raleigh, NC.

To my monsters,
Petra & Mathilda.

All profits from Ten Words are going to the NHS to pay for two of
the NICU incubators that saved Petra and Mathilda's lives.

More info at **Jeremy.live/tenwords**

This book was

inspired by...

the world's
greatest
marketer,

a Joker,

And two fake

presidents.

--- * ---

"If you can't state your position in less than eight words you don't have a position."

SETH GODIN

--- * ---

"Life is short. Act accordingly."

JACK NICHOLSON

--- * ---

"Ten word answers can kill you in politics. They're the tip of the sword."

PRESIDENT BARTLET

--- * ---

"We must tell our stories as fast and as compellingly as possible."

PRESIDENT UNDERWOOD

--- * ---

Life is short.

Act accordingly.

JACK NICHOLSON

Since 2008 Twitter has encouraged me to tell short stories in 140 characters...

... so I'd like to try and inspire you with 140 characters.

140 CHARACTERS

| WILL.I.AM ADAMS | ANGELA AHRENDTS | JESSICA ALBA | WOODY ALLEN |

HANS CHRISTIAN ANDERSEN — CHRIS ANDERSON — ARISTOTLE — P.T. BARNUM

 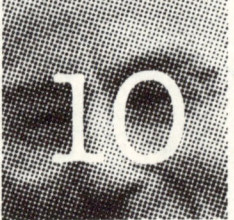 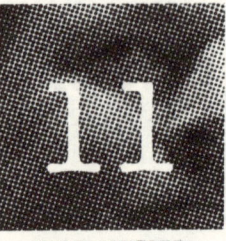 

BILLY BEANE — PETER BENENSON — MARC BENIOFF — TIM BERNERS-LEE

   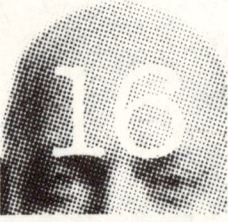

JEFF BEZOS — MICHAEL BLOOMBERG — BONO — DAVE BRAILSFORD

RICHARD BRANSON — BRENE BROWN — THOMAS BURBERRY — ANDREW CARNEGIE

DALE CARNEGIE

COCO CHANEL

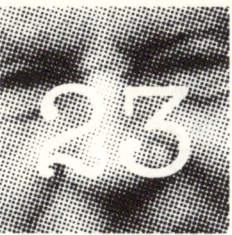
YVON CHOUINARD

CLAY CHRISTENSSEN

WINSTON CHURCHILL

PAULO COELHO

BRIAN COX

MARIE CURIE

MILES DAVIS

ROBERT De NIRO

W. EDWARDS DEMING

CHRISTIAN DIOR

WALT DISNEY

CORY DOCTOROW

JULIA DONALDSON

JACK DORSEY

NANCY DUARTE

ROBIN DUNBAR

BOB DYLAN

THOMAS EDISON

ALBERT EINSTEIN

JIMMY FALLON

JON FAVREAU

TIM FERRISS

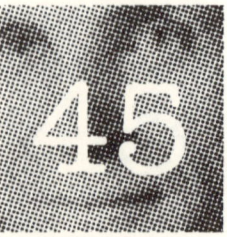
HENRY FORD

TOM FORD

BENJAMIN FRANKLIN

BILL GATES

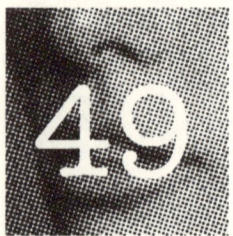
STEFANI GERMANOTTA

SETH GODIN

BILLY GRAHAM

TIM GROVER

TOM HANKS

TINKER HATFIELD

AUDREY HEPBURN

REID HOFFMAN

GRACE HOPPER

STEVE JOBS

KATHERINE JOHNSON

CHARLES "CHUCK" JONES

MICHAEL JORDAN

TRAVIS KALANICK

KEVIN KELLY

JOHN F. KENNEDY

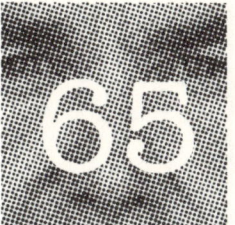
JEFF KOONS

JAN KOUM

HEDY LAMAR

JOHN LASSETER

ESTEE LAUDER

JOHN LENNON

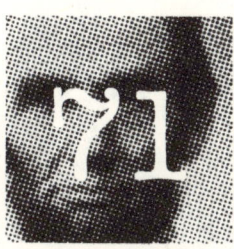
ABRAHAM LINCOLN

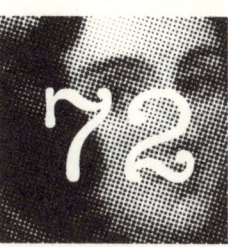
ADA LOVELACE

JACK MA

JOHN MACKAY

JOHN C. MAXWELL

LEE ALEXANDER McQUEEN

TAMARA MELLON

MARILYN MONROE

ELON MUSK

BLAKE MYCOSKIE

 81 SATYA NADELLA
 82 BARACK OBAMA
 83 DAVID OGILVY
 84 JAMIE OLIVER
 85 JIRO ONO
 86 GEORGE ORWELL
 87 JOEL OSTEEN
 88 GEORGE S. PATTON
 89 TOM PETERS
 90 MIUCCIA PRADA
 91 TONY ROBBINS
 92 KEVIN ROBERTS
 93 GINNI ROMETTY
 94 J.K. ROWLING
 95 BABE RUTH
 96 SHERYL SANDBERG
 97 CHARLES SCHULTZ
 98 JERRY SEINFELD
 99 RICARDO SEMLER
 100 JASON SILVA

NATE SILVER · RAF SIMONS · SIMON SINEK · WILL SMITH

PATTI SMITH · PAUL SMITH · THEODORE SORENSEN · AARON SORKIN

  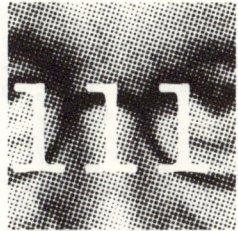 

KEVIN SPACEY · EVAN SPIEGEL · STEVEN SPIELBERG · ANDREW STANTON

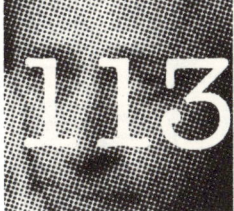   

JON STEWART · BIZ STONE · LEVI STRAUSS · VALENTINA TERESHKOCA

PETER THIEL · ALAN TURING · MARK TWAIN · GARY VAYNERCHUK

CEDRIC VILLANI

DITA VON TEESE

JEREMY WAITE

JOHNNIE WALKER

YUJA WANG

ANDY WARHOL

THOMAS J. WATSON Sr

BILL WATTERSON

JOSIAH WEDGWOOD

ERIC WEINSTEIN

ORSON WELLES

MAE WEST

VIVIENNE WESTWOOD

ROBIN WILLIAMS

JOCKO WILLINK

OPRAH WINFREY

ANNA WINTOUR

TERRY WOGAN

ZIG ZIGLAR

MARK ZUCKERBERG

"Just because you are a character, doesn't mean that you have character„.

WINSTON WOLFE

#TENWORDS

Attributes of a Story(teller).

When I first started working with Facebook commercially in 2010 they had just launched their brand platform. I was eager to build engaging brand pages on this new platform, so I started to learn everything I could about why people shared things on social media, what got shared the most and how it worked. The two things that I discovered continue to shape the way that I think about people and content today. The first thing I learned was that the most engaging social content revolves around what Facebook *likes* to call the four *passion pillars*:

1. Music
2. Fashion
3. Film / TV
4. Sport

With America's *Tweeter-in-Chief* posting daily sound-bite manifestos we should now probably add politics to that list as well, but for the most part, these are the brand categories that get shared the fastest. As I pondered these pillars, a wonderful thing happened. When I started to examine Facebook's most successful content within those categories. I discovered that in the majority of cases, the most engaging content did one (or more) of just six things. Three of them spoke to the heart (using emotion) and three of them appealed to the head (using logic). Brands are emotional and living entities. So when I understood that people engage with content and make important decisions with their hearts and then justify them with their heads, I knew I was on to something*.

 If you work in marketing or have any responsibility for creating, selling or distributing content that you want people to engage with and share, you might find that plotting your own content on a chart laid out like this is a very useful exercise. It's a fascinating process that helps you to see where the gaps in your content strategy are.

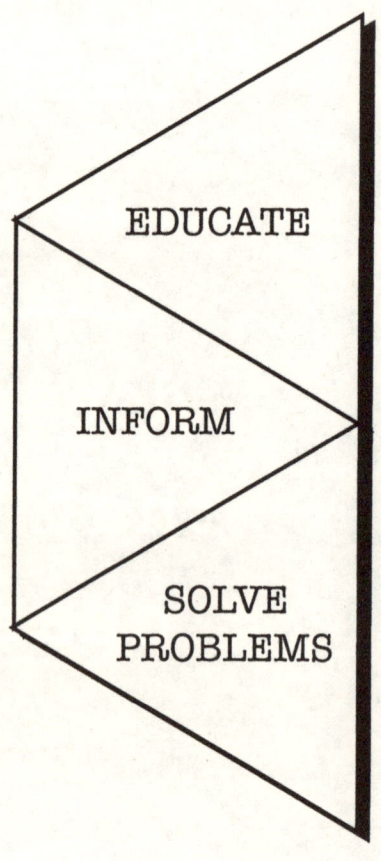

EDUCATE

INFORM

SOLVE PROBLEMS

For the
HEAD

---

* (I wrote 100,000 words on this topic in a previous book called "*From Survival to Significance*" which formed some of the research for *Ten Words*).

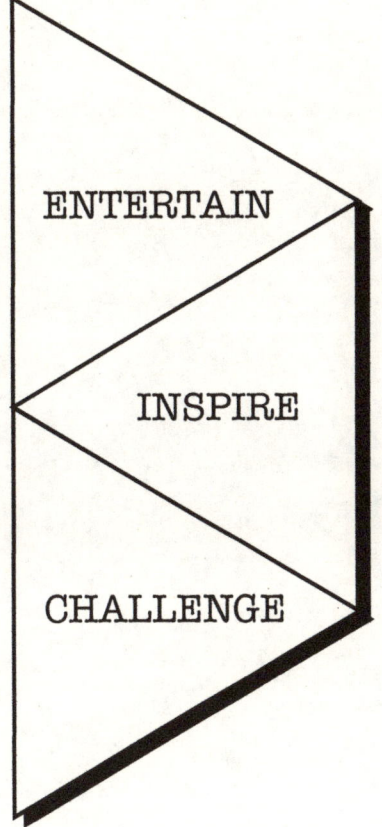

For the
HEART

During the process of writing *Ten Words*, I made the connection that the attributes of the most engaging people aren't all that different from the most engaging content. It's not just about their *Ten Words*, it's about how and why they said them. This book includes many people from the world of music, TV, fashion, film and sport and I find it fascinating that the attributes which make us love each of these people can also be defined by one of these six characteristics:

For the Head

EDUCATE – *"The Teachers"*
- Chris Anderson
- Professor Brian Cox
- Cedric Villani

INFORM – *"The Presenters"*
- Nate Silver
- W. Edwards Deming
- Robin Dunbar

SOLVE PROBLEMS – *"The Innovators"*
- Will.I.Am
- Thomas Edison
- Thomas Burberry

For the Heart

ENTERTAIN – *"The Entertainers"*
- Bono
- Kevin Spacey
- Aaron Sorkin

INSPIRE – *"The Leaders"*
- Marc Benioff
- Sir Richard Branson
- Michael Bloomberg

CHALLENGE – *"The Preachers"*
- Joel Osteen
- Simon Sinek
- Tony Robbins

Sorry I wrote you such a long ~~letter~~ sentence...

Why I Wrote Ten Words.

When I started my career as a marketer over twenty years ago, every business book that I read for inspiration or advice told me that I needed to have an *"elevator pitch"* – a short but powerful statement that explained in a clear and concise manner exactly what it was that I did. As a marketer, it was also my job to help other people find and write their own elevator pitches. A task much easier said than done. Some of the companies I worked with couldn't understand why it took me so long to write these short statements for them. I tried to explain how it was much easier to write a long wordy mission statement than it was to craft a good elevator pitch. Some people got it. Many didn't. And I hardly ever got paid for the actual amount of time it took me to write them. It wasn't long before I started to resent the lack of respect that some people had for this difficult process, because putting a price on a short sentence is hard. *Really* hard. It's like searching for a good idea for a new advertising campaign. Sometimes you have to slave away for weeks before you come up with something meaningful. Other times the idea mysteriously pops into your head unannounced at 3am in the morning, when you're on your way home from a heavy night out.

I always struggled to put a price on that process, because the best statements I came up with often seemed so obvious once I wrote them down. I sometimes felt guilty for charging for fifty hours work to produce what looked like a simple sentence or two that could have been written on a napkin during an afternoon in the pub. Simplifying complexity is hard work.

Ten years later, I realised my dream of founding a company when I set up a branding consultancy in Manchester in the north of England. Almost immediately I was fortunate to win a round of investment when I stumbled upon a prominent local businessman who liked my ideas. Our first meeting was in the lobby of a gorgeous hotel. I was quite nervous as I'd never been courted by an investor before. He sat me down, ordered us a coffee and tried to lull me into a false sense of security with some small talk before hitting me with the one question he suggested the future of my business (and our relationship) depended upon…

"So Jeremy, what's your elevator pitch?"

I remember bumbling a few words that were almost coherent, which explained to him how I wanted to build a *"relationship marketing agency"* that inspired brands with big ideas, small words and short sentences. I cringe thinking back to how naively I pitched my business, but miraculously it worked, and we were soon building an agency called *Juicy* with offices in Manchester, Bradford and London.

That was 2005.

Today, many things *have* changed, but some things have not changed at all. Advisors, banks, business authors and investors are *still* telling entrepreneurs and business leaders that they need an elevator pitch in order to pitch their purpose and their products.

But today, there's a problem.

Traditional elevator pitches don't work anymore.

The concept of an elevator pitch is good in principle. Conventional wisdom states that you basically have thirty seconds to describe what you do, why you do it, and why anyone should care. Nothing wrong with that in theory. The only problem today is that people don't have thirty seconds to listen to your pitch anymore. They sometimes don't even have twenty. In fact if you believe the research from some of today's top behavioural scientists and anthropologists, you'll find that the average person's attention span is now slightly less than that of a goldfish. That's somewhere between five and eight seconds. And based upon the speed at which the average person talks, that's roughly *ten words*.

Political speechwriter Jeremy Steffens has written many elevator pitches as a communications director to congressmen in the U.S. House of Representatives. Like any good marketer, Jeremy's brief was to write speeches for his clients, with the purpose of distilling their big ideas and manifestos into short media-friendly sound bites. He once told me that the biggest challenge in today's political landscape is that ten minute speeches, no matter how well written they are, or how articulately they are delivered, are usually always reduced to ten second video clips or ten word headlines. JFK and Barack Obama understood this more than their opponents when they were running for president. Their communications teams broke down their key manifestos into sound bites that were the length of the average person's attention span at the time, but more of that later in the book. Some marketers believe that this isn't true, that the way we tell stories hasn't changed for centuries and we shouldn't submit to popular demand by being forced to craft shorter messages that suit a generation that likes to tell stories in swipes. The first part of that statement is true, but to those who are still convinced that thirty second elevator pitches and wordy mission statements *still* work, I offer you some advice from one of the world's best short story tellers,

"*It ain't what you don't know that gets you into trouble. It's what you know for sure that just ain't so*". Mark Twain

So, as I see it, we basically have ten words to describe *what* we do, *why* we do it and *why* anyone should care.

#TENWORDS

If this *is* true, our challenge therefore lies in not just reducing the amount of words we use in order to appeal to dwindling attention spans, but in delivering the same power found in a longer statement in a much shorter sentence, without diluting its impact. Being able to give a thirty second elevator pitch is quite a luxury these days and not actually that hard to deliver if you have practiced and rehearsed it. But conveying that same amount of purpose and emotion in *less than* ten seconds, or ten words, is *very* hard. The world has evolved, and as my friend and mentor Brian Solis likes to say,

"It's no longer about survival of the fittest. It's about survival of the fastest".

That's why I wrote this little book. I wanted to showcase some brilliant ten word statements, manifestos and philosophies from some of the people who have inspired me the most. People who I have either spoken about in some of my keynotes or who I have been lucky enough to work with. But the one thing I wanted to make sure I didn't do was just create an interesting book of quotes that would no doubt look good on Instagram but probably end up as toilet reading! For *Ten Words* to be useful, I wanted to make sure that I showcased not just their ten word quotes (the world has enough books of quotations already – I think I own most of them), but I wanted to highlight some of the thinking behind their quotes. By giving some background, and directing you to a place where you can dig deeper to find out more, it is my hope that their words might also encourage you to find ways of telling you own story as fast and as compellingly as possible. I have been careful to lay out each page as simply as possible, whilst also being mindful that business people have attention spans of around seventy five seconds (according to my friend at Google) when flicking through business books. This is why each page tells a short 250 word story, inspired by each ten word quote, which takes around seventy five seconds to read. That seems deep enough to provide some context, but short enough to communicate each of these big ideas and statements into bite sized chunks.

Ten word statements sound easy. That's the beauty of them. But they're incredibly difficult to put together. Over the last few years I've worked at Adobe, Salesforce, Facebook and IBM with some of the largest brands in the world, and if there is one thing that all the brands I have worked with have in common (with no exceptions), it's that they all struggle to communicate their big ideas in small words and short sentences. One of my favourite writers and thinkers, the mathematician and theologian Blaise Pascal put it best when he said,

"Sorry I wrote you such a long letter, I didn't have time to write a shorter one".

#**TEN**WORDS

I've been thinking about this whole concept of ten words – big ideas, small words and short sentences ever since I started my career. I have spent more hours than any sensible person should, getting lost in book shops searching for books about quotes, pitches, vintage advertising, storyboarding or generally any book that talks about simplifying complicated things. On the occasions that I have discovered such treasure I snapped it up, building a small library in the process. Some of the best books I have collected on these topics over the last twenty years are over one hundred years old. But of the many beautiful books that I have bought (which much to my wife's dismay are real books rather than digital versions), none of them have quite hit on the simplicity of ten words. It's a cliché that many reluctant authors mention, but this really was a case of *"if no one else has written this book maybe I should..."*

We all have interesting stories to tell, and while this all seemed very fascinating to me, I wasn't sure if it would be interesting to anyone else, and for that reason I was initially very reluctant to write it down, let alone piece everything together to form a book. But I'm glad I did. Ten Words has changed the way that I think about many things, both personally and professionally and has inspired me to look beyond those Instagram-friendly ten words quotes, for a deeper meaning. Maybe *Ten Words* will also challenge you in some small way, who knows? I hope so. Anyway, thanks for picking it up. There are many things that you could be doing right now, but I'm honored that you chose to read this. Here's hoping that you'll enjoy reading it as much as I enjoyed writing it.

Carpe Diem!

Jeremy

GOV.UK

<25 Words

Research conducted by the UK digital government department discovered that sentences longer than 25 words aren't accessible. According to their official guidelines, whenever you are communicating a message to the general public if you have sentences longer than 25 words, you must try to break them up or condense them. If you can't, make sure they're in plain English because when you write more, people understand less. GOV.UK went on to explain how people distrust jargon and that being clear and direct helps - as do shorter sentences. Writing guru Ann Wylie describes research showing that when average sentence length is 14 words, readers understand more than 90% of what they're reading. At 43 words, comprehension drops to less than 10%. Studies also show that sentences of around **Ten Words** are considered easy to read, while those of 21 words are fairly difficult. At 25 words, sentences become difficult, and 29 words or longer, very difficult.

Long sentences aren't just difficult for people who struggle with reading or have a cognitive disability like dyslexia or attention deficit hyperactivity disorder. They're also a problem for highly literate people with extensive vocabularies. This is partly because people tend to scan, no read. In fact, most people only read around 25% of what's on a page. This means it's important to get information across quickly. Long, complicated sentences also force readers to slow down and work harder to understand what they're reading. This isn't something people want to do, even if they're familiar with the subject or language you're using. It's easy to assume this isn't the case for highly literate readers or people considered experts. Yet the more educated a person is, and the more specialist their knowledge, the more they want it in plain English. These people often have the least time and most to read. Which means they just want to understand your point and move on, quickly.

https://insidegovuk.blog.gov.uk/2014/08/04/sentence-length-why-25-words-is-our-limit/

"Since when did marketing become the 'Make It Pretty' department?"

(Why can't it be the 'Make It Better' department?)

What Inspired Ten Words?

Early in 2017 a number of very curious things happened which left me in no doubt that I was supposed to put all these thoughts together and write *Ten Words* myself. Every so often the stars seem to align and everything seems to slot into place. It doesn't happen very often, but when it does it's very inconvenient, and that's pretty much what happened to me. I had no plans to write a book, in fact I didn't even have any time to write a book. I'd recently become the father of two gorgeous twins (Petra and Mathilda) and had started a new job at IBM, but despite feeling like I already didn't have enough hours in each day, six seemingly random events in one week conspired against me, forcing me to think that I needed to find the time to put Ten Words onto paper. In order of appearance, these are the six happy coincidences which occurred to me between Friday, January 20th 2017 and 27th January. Serendipity at its finest.

1. I studied a research paper on neuroscience from Microsoft about the evolution of attention spans. Over the last fifty years, our attention span for media soundbites had dropped from just over thirty seconds to below ten seconds.
2. I analysed President Trump's inauguration speech and noticed many ten word answers. I also discovered that Trump's 1,433 word inauguration speech delivered in just over 16 minutes was equivalent to roughly ten words being delivered every 8 seconds.
3. I read a Seth Godin book which spoke about 8-10 word mission statements.
4. I found an old quote by Jack Nicholson about telling short stories in an old notebook which read, "*Life is short. Act accordingly*".
5. That week I was watching season four of the West Wing and unbeknown to me, the episode I was on, Episode 6 called "*Game On*" was an entire episode devoted to the phrase "*ten word answers*" which are used in political debates.
6. I wrote a personal business plan trying to describe my job simply to other IBMers. Many of my sentences were between nine and eleven words long.

Fascinated by all these coincidences I turned to the web to search for "*ten words*" and soon discovered a wonderful Twitter account called **@TenWordsPoem**. Never before had I seen such dramatic, sad, inspiring, thought provoking and often heart wrenching stories told in exactly ten words. I haven't approached the author for more context or background surrounding their tweets because I like the mystery that surrounds them. Poems, as with mission statements and elevator pitches, become more difficult to write the shorter they become. But as I am attempting to prove in this book, short sentences are far more memorable because they carry more emotional weight.

Here's a small selection of the tweets I saw when I read a few posts from @TenWordsPoem:

- *"I wonder what weight this fragile thread of connection carries".*
- *"The most selfish thing I'll ever do is love you".*
- *"I'm cursed with a heart that never ceases to love".*
- *"You're like the rain. An old friend with bad timing".*
- *"He spoke to her and then the world fell apart".*
- *"Your light will encapsulate entire cities once you let it".*
- *"The stars were never meant to find you a home".*
- *"What if no one else likes my sort of crazy?"*
- *"Trust me, I'm OK. I just wish I was dead".*
- *"I fell asleep chasing dreams and woke up an optimist".*

... and finally, my favourite,

"You can change the world just by sharing your story".

The entire twitter feed of @TenWordsPoem was full of stories and powerful emotions made up of small words. I read hundreds of them, captivated by the depth of emotions that came across in these short sentences. This is what marketing is supposed to be about. Communicating words and messages that reach into your heart, and make you feel something when you hear them, (and hopefully) inspire you to do something, buy something or share something with the people you care about. I was eager not to over-think this whole thing as I usually do, but it became apparent to me that this was a book which I needed to write as much as any audience needed to read it. It would have been easy to ignore these seemingly unconnected events and write them off as curious coincidences, but the more I thought about it, the more surreal the connection between these events seemed to me. All a bit too much of a co-incidence? Maybe. Maybe not. But what did I have to lose? I started to jot some ideas down as I looked to explore whether this had the potential to be a book instead of just a really long blog post!

No sooner had I received this epiphany and started to join the dots between these events, than I remembered a moment which shaped my career, and changed the way that I thought about marketing. It was a moment just like any other where I found myself in a boardroom discussing mission statements and campaign slogans, but unlike any meeting I had been involved in before, this meeting took a very different turn which nobody in the room expected. It was a couple of years ago and I was with a CEO who was assessing the value of his marketing team (or lack of).

#**TEN**WORDS

He had two teams. They had both produced good work by any standard. One had increased profits by 4%, the other had increased loyalty by 6% and reduced 'customer churn' by 7%. One focused on success, the other focused on influence. Both teams were successful by any marketing metric, but the CEO wasn't happy. He didn't feel like he was *making a difference*. He explained to those gathered in the room how he joined the company in order to inspire people and "*move the industry forward*". From his perspective, increasing profits, shareholder dividends and customer retention was not moving the company (or the industry forward), it was just doing good business. And then from nowhere, without any invitation or prior warning, a junior marketing executive stood up and walked over to a whiteboard which was sitting in the corner of the boardroom. This wasn't the kind of boardroom where you did that kind of thing. Especially not if you are a junior marketing assistant. It wasn't always a friendly environment and speaking out of turn could often have very career limiting implications. Still, this marketing manager only a few years out of university strolled across the room and without saying a word, he wrote down the figures from both teams of the whiteboard.

The marker didn't have much ink left and the squeak of him writing in silence, without anyone knowing what he was doing, was both awkward, bizarre and a bit surreal. The other executives looked at each other with raised eyebrows. On one side of the board he wrote the ROI (return on investment) figure taken from the profitable campaign that was being reviewed. On the other side he wrote the NPS (net promoter) score which showed an increase in customer lifetime value (a result of higher customer satisfaction from improving customer service during the campaign). The company had made $9M as a direct result of this marketing campaign. It was a campaign that would likely win some industry awards where team members would toast each others marketing prowess over some bottles of bubbles in a posh hotel somewhere. As it was, they were in a boardroom being challenged by their chief executive to find a third way. And that was when our junior marketing hero dropped his bombshell...

"$9M is a success. $8M would still be a success. But giving $1M to start a foundation that serves under-privileged kids would be significant. That kind of thinking would change the industry".*

Crossing out the $9M figure, he changed it to $8M and added a third column with $1M at the top. Over the next 3 minutes, he explained how $8M profit was still a strong number and the team would still be rock stars and all get their bonus. But what if they did something different? How incredible might it be if the profits from the campaign created the opportunity to fund a new foundation, such as educating teenage girls in Western Africa about health and fitness?

* (Not exactly ten words, but this encapsulates everything I want *Ten Words* to stand for. BIG ideas, delivered with small words in short sentences).

The idea for this initiative was not a new one, but nobody had found a way to pay for it, or a way to justify the expense. Our friend explained how this wasn't an expense, it was an *investment* from the marketing team. My jaw dropped. This twenty something executive had just, in one moment, raised $1M for a cause close to his heart and one relevant to the company, and aligned it to the vision of the CEO and the values of the business. The CEO smiled. He asked the senior marketers in the room if this was their idea. It wasn't. He asked why wasn't it. Needless to say the junior exec got a significant promotion, went on to build a team of his own and continues to be a meaningful marketer to this day. The beauty of this story is not just that marketers can make a real difference, but the fact that such a great idea came from the most junior person in the room. It was in that moment when I realised that all marketers can (and should) be held to a higher purpose. Of course they should be expected to write clever copy and deliver campaigns which are commercial successes. Of course marketers should build profitable or loyal relationships, but when they do their jobs well, as our friend very much did in this instance, marketers can build meaningful relationships as well. A very clever marketer once said, *"Since when did marketing become the 'make it pretty' department?"* I heard it was attributed to a CMO at Hewlett-Packard but couldn't find any proof. It doesn't matter, it's a great quote. But wouldn't it be better if marketing was the *'make it better'* department? That's a business unit I can proudly stand behind, and that's the kind of thinking I wanted to showcase in this book. Words that don't just sound pretty, but words which make a difference.

So, what you will find over the next few pages is not just an eclectic mix of influential people, but many marketers and storytellers who changed their industry in some way, inspiring those around them to think differently. The book includes scientists, astronauts, politicians, film directors, actors, comedians and fashion designers. Some of the people you will meet on these pages, like Mark Zuckerberg, Steve Jobs, Peter Thiel, Josiah Wedgwood, John Mackey, Vivienne Westwood and Henry Ford, all have *ten word* sentences to give their lives purpose, stand for something or change their industry in some way. Others became famous for ten word quotes and may have never intentionally thought to communicate their visions and big ideas in small words and short sentences. Either way, I hope that the collection of stories which I have curated in ten words, challenge you to think differently about your life and your career. Each of their stories can be read in less than two minutes (the average attention span of a busy executive) so hopefully, no matter how busy you are, you will find the time to dip in and out of this book and find yourself being inspired by some wonderful people. It is my hope that their stories don't just inspire you to do something cool and profitable, but they encourage you to do something meaningful as well.

#TENWORDS

THE REVOLUTION WILL BE LED BY A 12-YEAR-OLD GIRL

IF YOU WANT TO END POVERTY AND HELP THE DEVELOPING WORLD, THE BEST THING YOU CAN DO IS INVEST TIME, ENERGY, AND FUNDING INTO ADOLESCENT GIRLS. IT'S CALLED THE GIRL EFFECT, BECAUSE GIRLS ARE UNIQUELY CAPABLE OF INVESTING IN THEIR COMMUNITIES AND MAKING THE WORLD BETTER. BUT HERE ARE 10 THINGS THAT STAND IN THEIR WAY:

1. LET'S SEE SOME ID
Without a birth certificate or an ID, a girl in the developing world doesn't know and can't prove her age, protect herself from child marriage, open a bank account, vote, or eventually get a job. That makes it hard to save the world.

2. ILLITERACY DOES NOT LOOK GOOD ON A RESUME...
70% of the world's out-of-school children are girls. Girls deserve better. They deserve quality education and the safe environments and support that allow them to get to school on time and stay there through adolescence.

3. ...AND PREGNANCY DOESN'T LOOK GOOD ON A LITTLE GIRL
Child marriages are the norm in many cultures where girls' bodies aren't considered their own property. Pregnancy is the leading cause of death for girls 15-19 years old. Girls have a right to be able to protect their health and their bodies.

4. THE FACE OF HIV IS INCREASINGLY YOUNG AND FEMALE
When girls are educated about HIV, they stand a better chance of protecting themselves. But education is not enough. Girls need to be empowered and supported to make their own choices.

5. A NICE PLACE TO WORK WOULD BE NICE
If girls have the skills for safe and decent work, if they understand their rights, if they are financially literate and considered for nontraditional jobs at an appropriate age, if they get their fair share of training and internships, they will be armed and ready for economic independence.

6. THE CHECK IS IN THE MAIL, BUT IT'S GOING TO YOUR BROTHER
LESS THAN TWO CENTS of every international aid dollar is directed to girls. And yet when a girl has resources, she will reinvest them in her community at a much higher rate than a boy would. If the goal is health, wealth, and stability for all, a girl is the best investment.

7. ADOLESCENT GIRLS AREN'T JUST "FUTURE WOMEN"
They're girls. They deserve their own category. They need to be a distinct group when we talk about aid, education, sports, civic participation, health, and economics. Yes, they are future mothers. But they actually live in the present.

8. LAWS WERE MADE TO BE ENFORCED
Girls need advocates to write, speak up, lobby, and work to enforce good laws and change discriminatory policies.

9. SHE SHOULD BE A STATISTIC
We won't know how to help girls until we know what's going on with them. Hey, all you governments and NGOs and social scientists: You're accountable! We need an annual girl report card for every country so we can keep track of which girls are thriving and which girls are not.

10. EVERYONE GETS ON BOARD OR WE'RE ALL OVERBOARD
Boys, girls, moms, dads. If we don't all rally to support girls, nothing is going to change. Not for them, and not for us. Change starts with you. So get going.

girleffect.org

Great example of a campaign driven by the marketing team at Nike who helped to re-allocate profits towards this meaningful project.

What's next?

A TV show
inspired this
book with a
story about
ten words...

--- The West Wing ---

"Game On" ~ Episode 6 Season 4
[Show ID: 73] Presidential Debate
Written by *Aaron Sorkin*
Directed by *Alex Graves*
First aired 30th October 2002

CUT TO: INT. AUDITORIUM - NIGHT

MODERATOR ~ "Governor Ritchie, many economists have stated that the tax cut, which is centre piece of your economic agenda, could actually harm the economy. Is now really the time to cut taxes?"

RITCHIE ~ "You bet it is. We need to cut taxes for one reason -- the American people know how to spend their money better than the federal government does".

MODERATOR ~ "Mr. President, your rebutal".

BARTLET "There it is".

CUT TO: INT. SPIN ROOM - CONTINUOUS

REPORTER MARK ~ "What the hell?"

C.J. ~ "He's got it".

BARTLET [on TV] "That's the ten-word answer my staff's been looking for for two weeks.

There it is.

#TENWORDS

Ten-word answers can kill you in political campaigns.

They're the tip of the sword.

Here's my question: "What are the next ten words of your answer?" Your taxes are too high? So are mine.

Give me the next ten words. How are we going to do it? Give me ten after that, I'll drop out of the race right now.

Every once in a while... every once in a while, there's a day with an absolute right and an absolute wrong, but those days almost always include body counts. Other than that, there aren't very many unnuanced moments in leading a country that's way too big for ten words.

I'm the President of the United States, not the President of the people who agree with me. And by the way, if the left has a problem with that, they should vote for somebody else".

----- * -----

---

* As soon as I watched this episode, I knew that I had to write Ten Words. Despite the fact that this show aired 15 years ago, the message in this scene sums up perfectly the many things that are wrong with our governments, business leaders, politicians, journalists and marketers. Especially marketers. Whether it is a campaign headline, a manifesto pledge or an advertising slogan, putting anything into ten words is difficult. But finding the next ten words to back up your position, or the ten words after that to explain what you stand for - *that's* the real challenge.

The West Wing, Episode 6 Season 4 – **"Game On"** (Ten Words).

THE WEST WING
CREATED BY AARON SORKIN

Some of the companies I most admire, built their brands upon ten words.

#TENWORDS

For example...

The
world's leading
charity only
needs ten words
to explain its
purpose.

#TENWORDS

To create lasting solutions to poverty, hunger and social injustice.

(10 WORDS)

OXFAM

Oxfam is one of the world's leading providers of aid in humanitarian emergencies. In 2014–15, it supported more than 8 million people in crisis. Whenever and wherever there is a widespread threat to people's life and security, Oxfam will respond where it believes it can make a positive difference.

OXFAM

#TENWORDS

THE WORLD'S 85 RICHEST PEOPLE OWN THE SAME WEALTH AS THE 3.5 BILLION POOREST PEOPLE.

TOGETHER, WE CAN END EXTREME INEQUALITY.
TOGETHER, WE CAN EVEN IT UP.

JOIN US AT
WWW.OXFAM.ORG.UK/EVEN

EVEN IT UP | OXFAM

The world's fastest growing tech company is 'driven' by ten words.

#**TEN**WORDS

Provide transportation as reliable as running water. Everywhere. For everyone.

(10 WORDS)

UBER

Founded on a Parisien street corner in 2008, Uber soon became the world's fastest growing tech company. With its aggressive growth strategy and a co-founder (ex-CEO Travis Kalanick) who who embraced litigation as part of it's business model, Uber openly admits to wanting to "*destroy*" the competition rather than compete with them. Their ethics (or lack of) have caught up with them recently, but there is still no doubt that they pioneered a new way of doing business.

#TENWORDS

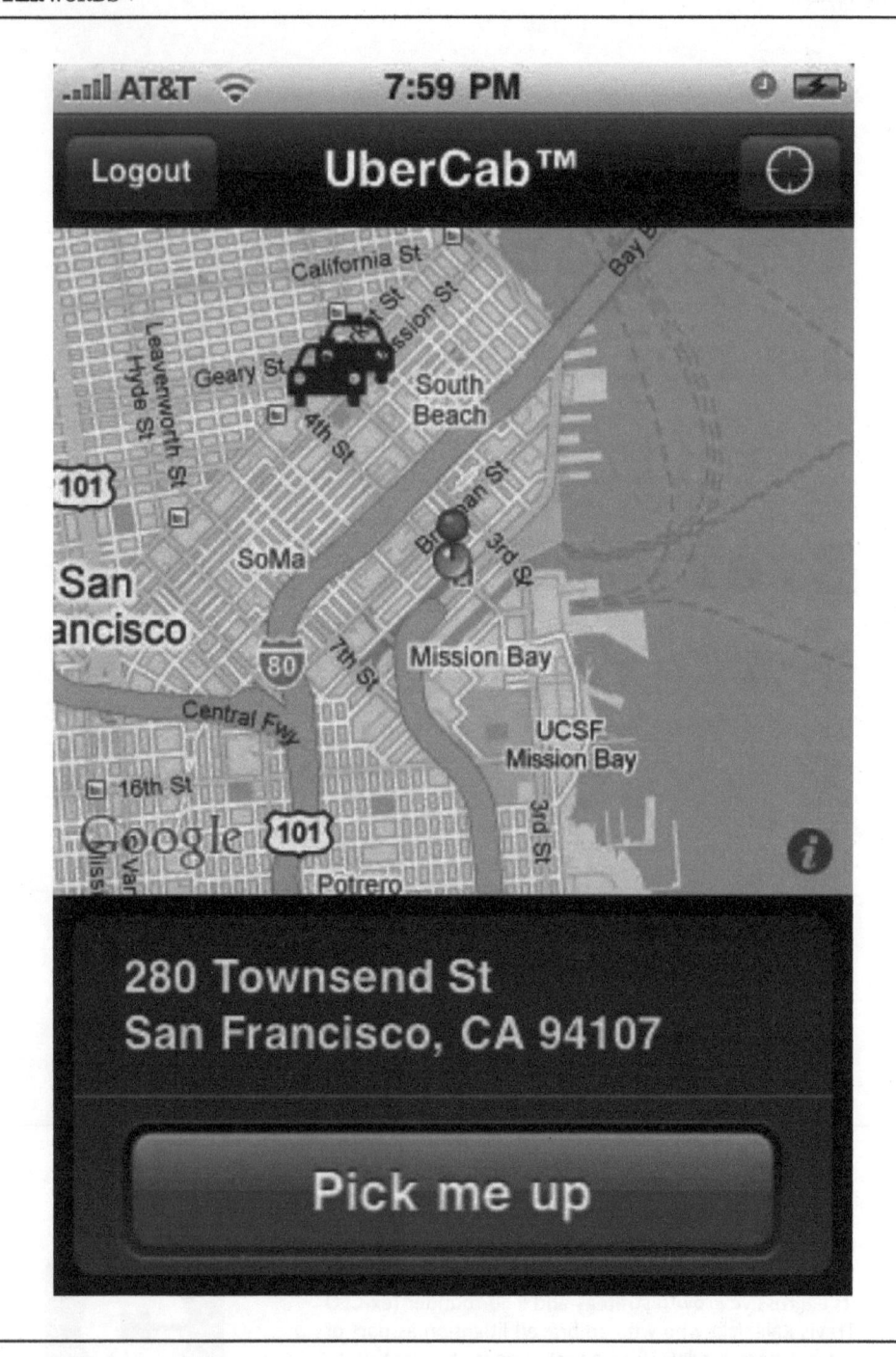

This is the first screenshot from Uber co-founder Travis Kalanick's cellphone, when Uber only had two cars on the road. Today there are over one million. When Travis first launched under the name UberCab for 100 of his closest friends, they each had to text him for a code in order to request one of his S-Class Mercedes.

The world's most valuable brand was built upon ten words.

#TENWORDS

A computer revolution is starting.

We can't get left behind.

(10 WORDS)

APPLE $AAPL

Interbrand ranking: 1
Market Capitalisation: $693 Bn
Founded: 1975

The world's most valuable brand was founded in Steve Jobs parents garage in 1975 with $1,350 from the sale of Jobs' VW and Wozniak's Hewlett-Packard calculator. The fear of missing out on a "revolution" and the opportunity to challenge IBM with Steve Jobs' marketing skills and Woz's engineering talent was all the motivation they needed.

When Steve Jobs returned to Apple in 1997 he needed a short sentence which inspired employees and re-ignited the brand, since it was just three months away from bankruptcy. After about thirty drafts, he came up with a fourteen word statement.

But he was Steve Jobs.

You're not.

You're only allowed ten...

#**TEN**WORDS

We must provide relevant and compelling solutions that customers can **only get from** Apple.

(14 WORDS)

Standing in front of the marketing team for the first time since returning to Apple, Jobs was frustrated that the marketing team of the world's most emotional company wasn't emotional anymore. *"The products suck. There is no sex in them anymore*"* he said. Jobs then scribbled fourteen words on the whiteboard making sure that everyone in the room was in no doubt as to what Apple's new mission was going to be.

*(10 WORDS)

STEVE JOBS is the most influential CEO of all time. Returning to the company that he was fired from in 1997, Apple's cash reserves placed the company less than 3 months away from bankruptcy. It had too many products. Jobs canned most of them and set up a new engineering team to work on *"Project Purple"*. That team invented the iPhone and within 14 years, Steve had turned Apple into the world's most valuable brand valuing the company at over $750 Billion.

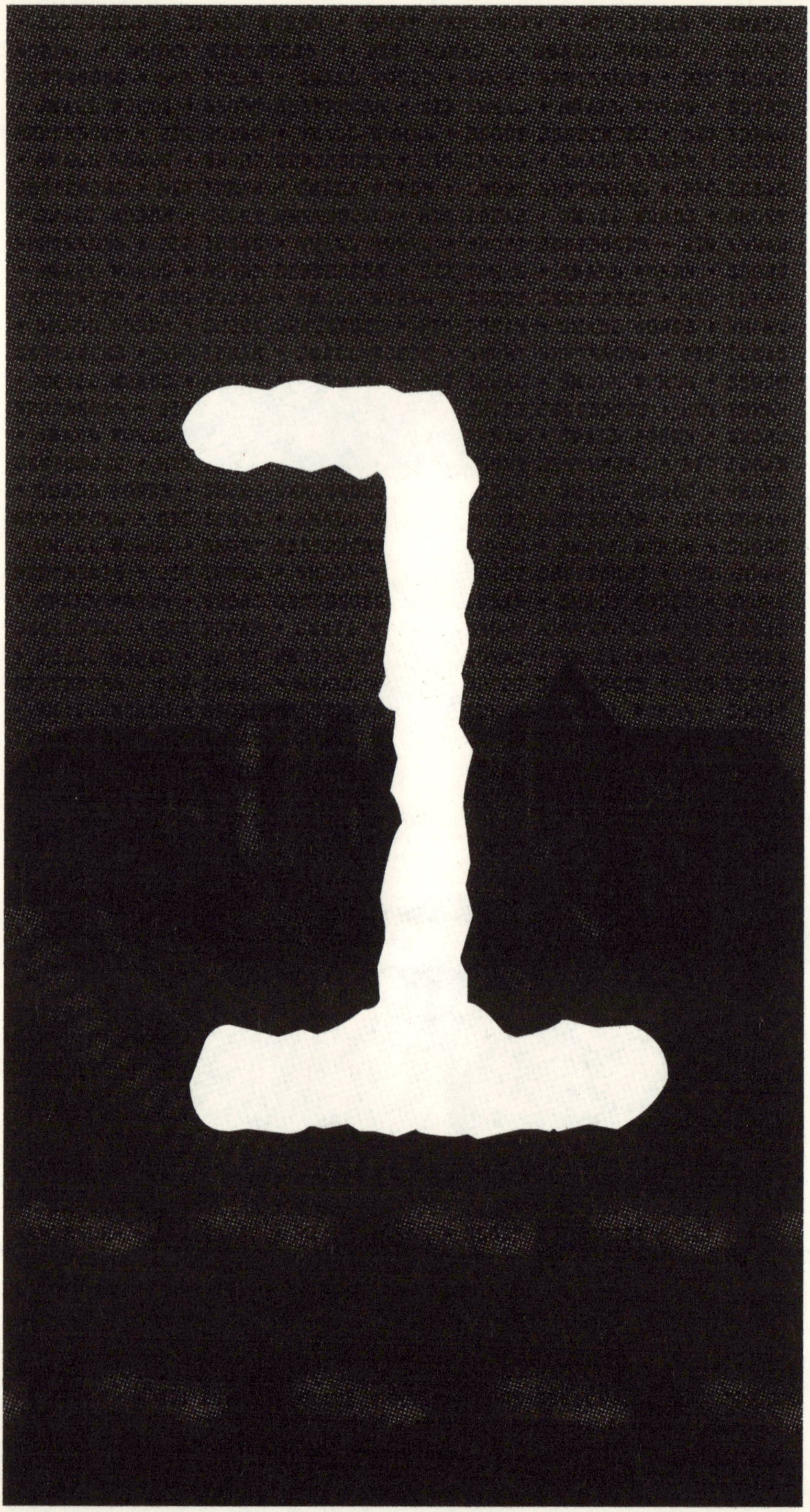
1

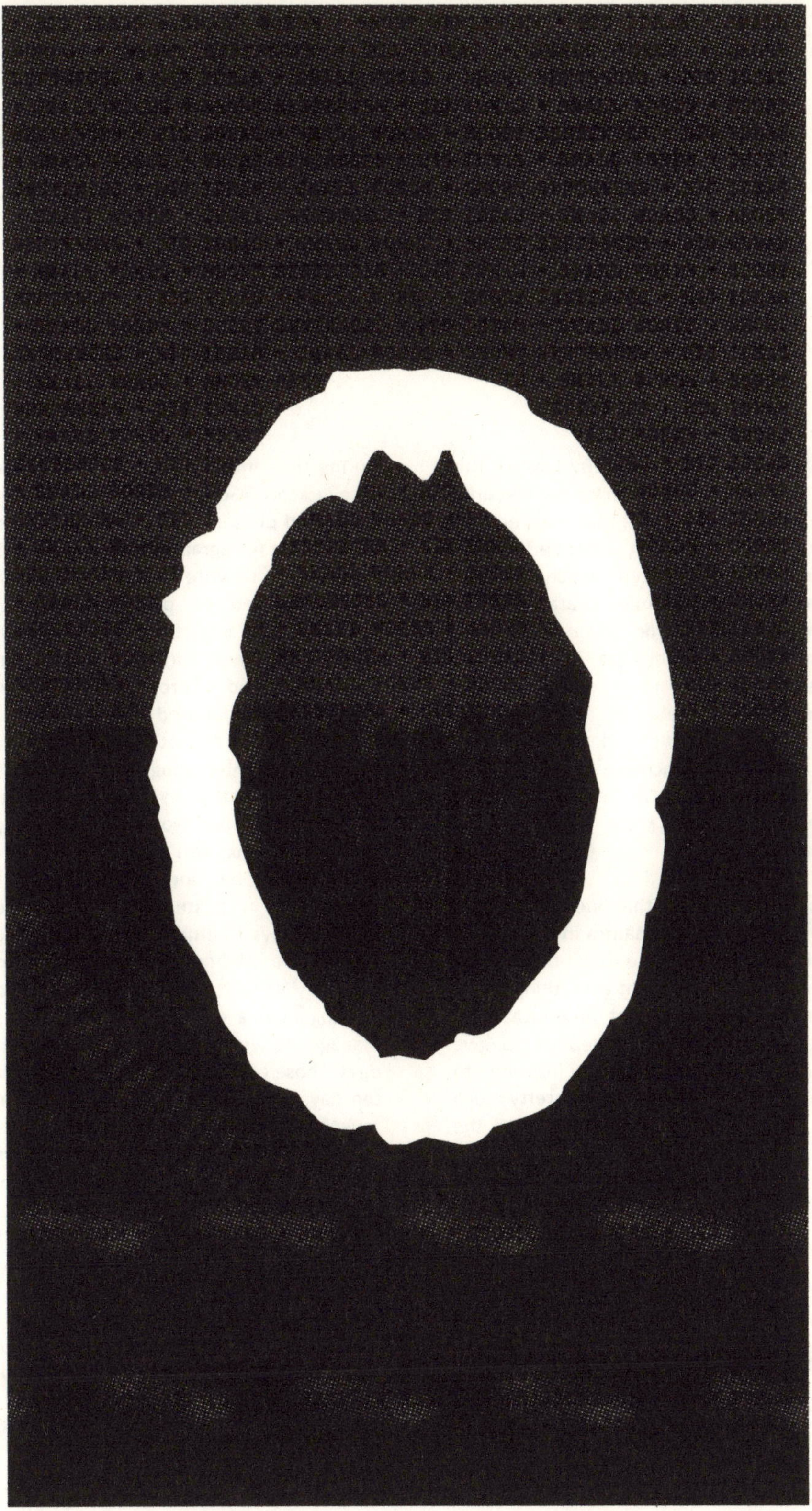

How I Wrote Ten Words.

If the West Wing inspired *why* I wrote this book, it was another show from my favourite screenwriter Aaron Sorkin that inspired *how* I wrote it. During an episode of The Newsroom, there is a scene which reaches a climax when the two main characters (Will McAvoy and Charlie Skinner), both journalists of the highest integrity, are discussing how they used to do the news differently. Desperate to cast off the restrictions that the network was placing on them in a race to increase ratings, Charlie turns to Will and says, "*In the old days we did the news well. You know how? We just decided to*".

Ever since I first heard that line it has stayed with me, almost like a mantra in the back of my mind that reminds me to get things done and not procrastinate. Not everything needs an elaborate plan, an agent, an education, a certain qualification or somebody to give you permission. Sometimes you just need to decide to do something. That's pretty much what happened with this book. I had the inspiration from all the random events I described earlier, and I also had the motivation as I had just finished reading *The First 90 Days* by Michael Watkins, which spoke about how productive leaders (especially new presidents and prime ministers) make 90-100 day plans to get things done. The first one hundred days are more important than any other time in office as they lay the foundations for all the important things which need to get done.

During this time I was following my friend Julia Jackson @SouthernMonkey who posts a numbered photograph based upon a theme each day on Instagram. So, I not only made a 100 day plan to write a book, but inspired by her, I decided to post one photo on Instagram each day of my progress, in order to keep me honest and help motivate me to get it finished. Throughout those one hundred days I doubted myself many times, mostly whether or not anyone else would find this stuff interesting, but the process of writing *Ten Words* soon became so cathartic, that I soon stopped worrying what anybody else might think. You can see how I wrote *Ten Words* by looking back at the photographs I posted during those one hundred days (during March 12th and June 22nd) with a brief commentary on Instagram @JeremyWaite. It took a bit of discipline and juggling a job, a wife and my twins, but I still managed to write *Ten Words* in one hundred days. Those one hundred days were basically ten days of planning, ten days of research, seventy days of writing and ten days of editing. I did it as much to prove to myself that it could be done, as to challenge others that they could do the same. It's amazing what you can do when you put your mind to something that you "*just decided to*".

"Do what you can, with what you have, where you are".

Theodore Roosevelt

#TENWORDS

#**TEN**WORDS

WILL.I.AM ADAMS

"Look at the world. See the problem. And solve it".

Will.I.Am is passionate about teaching under-privileged kids to code. He had very few possessions and no computer growing up but didn't consider himself *"poor"*. He only realised he might be poor when he volunteered to help with a food drive, and discovered his friends delivering the food that they collected to his own house that evening.

READ: *Will.I.Am*: The Unauthorized Biography
WATCH: His keynote at Dreamforce 2015
FOLLOW: @IAmWill | @codeorg

There is a fine line between genius and madness. In Will.I.Am's case, it's often hard to tell the difference. One minute he is talking about a new technology he's discovered, the next he is rapping with words you've never heard before! I first met the Black Eyed Pea's megastar at a marketing conference in Atlanta. Listening to him speak with journalists, I could sense his frustration, because it seemed like as soon as he opened his mouth his mind was already racing towards an entirely different subject. He can appear rude to those who don't understand him, but he is just thinking about things a bit faster than the rest of us. He told a small group of us, *"I've got all this stuff in my head at the same time as I'm doing stuff and I don't know how to stop or slow down"*.

Will.I.Am lives in LA in the most technologically advanced bunker you can imagine. He calls it "*The Future*" because he enjoys saying "*Welcome to The Future*" when you arrive! It is here that he works on projects ranging from smart watches and voice recognition software, to streaming songs from the surface of Mars and designing for Lexus. Each of these projects is linked by his desire to *"invent the future"*. He has had his fair share of successes *and* failures but he refuses to spend time reminiscing. Instead he stays optimistic by relying on a one sentence philosophy, **"Let's stop worrying about the past and go invent the future..."**

#TENWORDS

WILL.I.AM ADAMS

i.am+

809 N Cahuenga Blvd.
Los Angeles, CA 90038
+1 (323)210-3842

Tips for maximizing your interview time with will.i.am:

-Your access to The Future is for you alone (one person only). We regret that relatives, friends, interns and such cannot participate with you.

-Assume he will know exactly who you are and what you write about - no need to go into details about your outlet or personal background. He will also know that you will have seen a product demo prior to the interview. A member of the PR team will introduce you. Say hello, sit down and get started!

-Questions should be one sentence, straightforward questions. Refrain from editorializing about the subject/theme prior to asking a question that will clutter the conversation. Do not ask him to react to what other outlets have written about him in the past. If he asks you to repeat or restate a question, this indicates that you need to ask crisper, more direct questions.

-Have your list of questions in hand and keep an eye on it as the interview progresses. He will often answer multiple questions in one reply. Once you have captured the information, avoid asking questions that will require repeating the same information already shared.

-Start off with 1 - 2 warm up questions, and then get to the heart of what you really want to ask. Because he can sometimes give very lengthy responses, don't hold your most important questions until the end of your time allocation. Due to a tight rotation schedule, we will ask that journalists stick to time blocks as assigned for the day.

-If you need to get short answers to certain questions, bundle them in a "lightening round" toward the end of the interview, and be clear that one word, or very short answers are what you need. Fact Checking Basics:

Will.I.Am's mind operates with such speed that in order for journalists to keep up, his PR team encourage anyone preparing to interview him to use single words answers and very short sentences.

#TENWORDS

ANGELA AHRENDTS

"We live by what we believe, not what we see".

"I don't want to be a great chief executive without being a great mum and a great wife".

Angela Ahrendts is the senior vice president of Apple Retail tasked with increasing Apple's footprint as the world's most profitable retail brand, blessed with one of the world's highest NPS (customer satisfaction) scores.

READ: Angela Ahrendts' posts on Linkedin
WATCH: Angela Ahrendts - TEDx Hollywood (2013)
FOLLOW: @AngelaAhrendts

When Angela Ahrendts was the CEO of Burberry, its brand value was declining and sales were hovering at around $2 billion. By the time she left for her dream job to lead retail operations at Apple, Burberry's value rose to over $7 billion. Not too shabby. Shareholders rewarded her with a salary of around $26 million. Today she is the only female senior executive at Apple, earning even more than the CEO at just over $70 million per year. It's easy to be impressed by those numbers but Angela's salary is just representative of her meteoric rise as one of the world's most successful executives. She is often asked what she attributes her success to, and she always replies with the same sentiment, *"Trust your instincts and emotions. Let them guide you in every situation; they will not fail you"*.

Unlike many executives who rely on logic and data-driven arguments to run their business, Angela runs hers with her heart. Inspired by words from the great American poet Maya Angelou, Angela often recites her favourite quote, *"People will forget what you said, people will forget what you did, but people will never forget how you made them feel"*. It is this sentiment that Angela is embedding into the heart of Apple's retail division where she also likes to remind employees constantly of Simon Sinek's quote, *"The goal in business is not to sell to people who need what you have, but to work with people who believe what you believe"*.

#**TEN**WORDS

JESSICA ALBA

"If you look confident enough you can pull off anything".

Jessica Alba believes that she should constantly challenge herself and learn new things, which is why she tells people that *"Every five years I feel like I'm a completely different person"*.

Jessica Alba co-founded The Honest Company in 2011, an eco-friendly cosmetics company that doesn't use any unnecessary or potentially harmful chemicals. After becoming a mum in 2008, she struggled to find alternative products for her daughter who suffered allergic reactions to all the products that other mums recommended. Noticing a small gap in the market Jessica decided to do something about it. She was initially advised to start small by focusing on one product but she was determined to launch her company with 17!

Honest now boasts an impressive valuation of almost $2Bn, but it took a strong will to get her there, often ignoring the advice of people who she loved and respected. Everyone advised her to stick to the tried and tested celebrity formula of being the face of a new perfume or producing a signature clothing line. Instead, Jessica fixed her focus on creating a subscription based e-commerce business. Everyone around her said it was a bad idea. In the world of entertainment where celebrities are represented in 5 second sound-bites, Jessica wanted to create something more long-lasting. Nobody took her seriously but it just gave her the fire to move forward and prove everyone wrong. It took her a few years to eventually find her perfect business partners but throughout that time, and some very tough meetings, she relied on this ten word mantra to stay focused on her mission.

READ: *The Honest Life* by Jessica Alba
WATCH: Her keynote at Dreamforce 2015
FOLLOW: @JessicaAlba

#**TEN**WORDS

WOODY ALLEN

"Talent is luck. The important thing in life is courage".

Ever the wordsmith, Woody was recently asked to explain his 80% quote. *"The figure seems high to me today,"* Woody said, *"but I knew it was more than 60 and the extra syllable in 70 ruins the rhythm of the quote, so I think we should let it stand at 80".*

Woody Allen (king of the one liner) boasts credits as an actor, a director, a comedian, a musician and a writer. He is one of the most talented people in show business but he is always the first one to say that talent is not enough. Lots of people have talent, but very few *"show up"* and are courageous enough to make something happen. It is this idea of *"showing up"* which Woody is famous for. During an interview he was once giving to aspiring playwrights, he shared the now iconic quote *"80% of success is turning up"*. It's a line I have used at conferences many times myself, suggesting that regardless of the speakers or the quality of the content, good things often happen just by putting smart people in a room together.

Woody has made a career out of showing up. Over six decades he has been nominated for an Oscar® a total of 23 times: 15 as a screenwriter, 7 as a director, and once as an actor. Many film critics attribute his success to the fact that he is not commercially driven. *"If my films don't show a profit, I know I'm doing something right"*, he once said. Oscar® winners such as Diane Keaton claim he is the world's finest *"actor's director"* due to his ability to direct the most powerful scenes using the minimum amount of words. In a world where lengthy directions and long monologues are the norm, Woody has achieved great success simply by showing up, with a good script, a big idea, and a few one liners.

READ: The script for *"Hannah and Her Sisters"*.
WATCH: Woody Allen: a Documentary
FOLLOW: @WoodyAllen *(Although he never tweets).*

#**TEN**WORDS

HANS CHRISTIAN ANDERSEN

"Life itself is the most wonderful kind of fairy tale".

"Life is like a beautiful melody, only the lyrics are messed up".

Hans Christian Anderson wrote the words which send millions of children to sleep every night. He wrote many plays, novels, travel books and poems, but he is best known for the 212 fairy tales he wrote. His tales including *The Little Mermaid* and *The Ugly Duckling* have been translated into over 150 languages.

READ: One of his fairy tales to someone you love
WATCH: *The Little Mermaid*
FOLLOW: *#HansChristianAndersen*

Hans Christian Andersen is one of the finest tellers of short stories the world has ever seen. When he was younger, his first passion was to become an actor since everyone told him that he had such a beautiful singing voice, so it wasn't until he was 29 that he penned his first fairy tale. His early ambitions molded a great portion of his work. One of the things I love the most about Hans is that he wrote mostly about subjects he knew about. Andersen's own life for example, has been likened to that of the Ugly Duckling, who is born humbly amongst the ducks yet blossoms into a swan. Born the son of a poor cobbler, Hans became rich from his writing and famous throughout the world, although he suffered a great deal on his journey to wealth and happiness. It was those darker experiences that shaped many of his fairy tales which, when read in their original versions, are far more sophisticated than just mere children's fables. His personal struggles with his peers and idols during his formative years are recorded as a commentary on human nature and the society to which he was subjected. Sometimes this manifests itself as optimism, where goodness and beauty triumph, other times it is pessimism where the end is inevitable. In either instance, Andersen identifies with the downtrodden and oppressed. The fact that he is remembered as the storyteller who has made the world smile by drawing on his own tumultuous experiences is testament to his status as a literary master craftsman.

#TENWORDS

CHRIS ANDERSON

"People don't come to a talk to be sold to".

Each year 25,000 people apply to give an official TED talk but only a few hundred are chosen, such is Chris's commitment to only have the best speakers presenting at his $5,000 a seat conference. Giving a TED talk is such a big deal that people such as Ev Williams from Twitter have turned away millions of dollars from selling an idea, in favour of speaking about it at TED. I love Chris because he is a champion of big ideas, small words and short sentences, insisting that every TED talk lasts no longer than 18 minutes. And to make sure that all TED talks are both short *and* great, Chris asks speakers to learn the *"The Ten TED Commandments"* and promise not to break any of them!

1. Thou shalt not simply trot out thy usual shtick.
2. Thou shalt dream a great dream, or show forth a wondrous new thing, or share something thou hast never shared before.
3. Thou shalt reveal thy curiosity and thy passion.
4. Thou shalt tell a story.
5. Thou shalt freely comment on the utterances of other speakers for the sake of blessed connection and exquisite controversy.
6. Thou shalt not flaunt thine ego. Be thou vulnerable. Speak of thy failure as well as thy success.
7. Thou shalt not sell from the stage: neither thy company, thy goods, thy writings, nor thy desperate need for funding; lest thou be cast aside into outer darkness.
8. Thou shalt remember all the while: laughter is good.
9. Thou shalt not read thy speech.
10. Thou shalt not steal the time of them that follow thee.

Chris Anderson has revolutionised the traditional conference format by taking over a small Technology, Education and Design conference in 2002 and turning it into the TED organisation which has now delivered over 8,000 events and 60,000 talks (tickets to TED global sell out a year in advance). Twitter co-founder Evan Williams even turned down $1M for one of his projects once just because it meant he wouldn't have been able to give a TED talk.

READ: *TED Talks* by Chris Anderson
WATCH: TED.com
FOLLOW: @TEDchris | @TEDtalks

#TENWORDS

ARISTOTLE

"To avoid criticism: do nothing, say nothing and be nothing".

Commenting on Aristotle's rules for storytelling, Aaron Sorkin said that, *"Rules are what makes art beautiful"*, but knowing that all rules are also made to be broken, it's worth considering Steven Spielberg's perspective, *"People have forgotten how to tell a story. Stories don't have a middle or an end anymore. They usually have a beginning that never stops beginning"*.

READ: *Poetics* by Aristotle
WATCH: *Masterclass.com* with Aaron Sorkin
FOLLOW: @Aristotle

I have always been *aware* of Aristotle, but it was only when I did a screenwriting course with Aaron Sorkin that I discovered exactly how important Aristotle was to storytellers. Sorkin described Aristotle to me as *"the Greek God of Storytelling"* and directed me towards Aristotle's *Poetics*, arguably the most important piece of writing on storytelling ever published. In *Poetics*, Aristotle explains the necessity for every good plot to consist of three acts, but contrary to popular belief, these three acts are not simply a beginning a middle and an end. The three act structure refers to Aristotle's rules for storytelling:

- Act I: **Resolution** *(Introduction)*
- Act II: **Confrontation** *(Rising action)*
- Act III: **Resolution** *(Falling action)*

Deeper inspection of Aristotle's rules reveal that all good stories also have three scientific elements, affectionately known as the three keys of persuasion: *Pathos* (emotional stories), *Logos* (logical analysis) and *Ethos* (credible evidence). What I love about this philosophy is that it appeals to the head *and* the heart. It is also a model as relevant today as it was 2,000 years ago. When I worked with Facebook one of the first things I learned was that all good content should do three things: Inspire and Entertain (*Pathos*), Educate and Inform (*Logos*) and Challenge or Solve Problems (*Ethos*). I think Aristotle would have *"liked"* Facebook!

#TENWORDS

P.T. BARNUM

"The noblest art is that of making other people happy".

"Whatever you do, do it with all your might. Work at it, early and late, in season and out of season, not leaving a stone unturned, and never deferring for a single hour that which can be done just as well now".

P.T. Barnum *(The self-appointed 'Prince of Humbug')*

READ: The Art of Money Getting by P.T. Barnum
WATCH: P.T. Barnum by Evan Carmichael
FOLLOW: In someone else's footsteps (not Barnum's)

P.T. Barnum was a showman and a scoundrel. Regarded by many as one of the greatest marketers of all-time for his promotional skills and ability to attract an audience, Barnum was a man of few ethics. He was probably one of the greatest marketers of all-time, but not in a good way. Famous for coining the phrase, *"There's a sucker born every minute"*, Phineas Taylor Barnum made a fortune from his Bailey & Barnum travelling circus by promoting acts that didn't exist. Being an unscrupulous marketer is one thing (there are still many of those around today), but the fact that Barnum was so blatantly proud of the success that his devious marketing schemes brought, made him a remarkable character.

So proud was he of his success that he even published a book about his exploits in 1880 entitled *"The Art of Money Getting"*. In it he encouraged the marketing entrepreneurs of his day to follow his example because, *"Without promotion, something terrible happens... NOTHING!"* Unethical Barnum may have been but he justified his actions by believing that, *"Fortune always favors the brave, and never helps a man who does not help himself"*. I remember discussing this attitude and the ethics of marketing with Samsung CMO Marc Mathieu. His response encapsulated perfectly what marketing should *really* be about, *"Marketing used to be about creating a myth and selling it; Now it's about finding a truth and sharing it".*

#TENWORDS

P.T. BARNUM

Many of Barnum's most popular acts were nothing but hoaxes, but he made boatloads of money off them, even after they were exposed as frauds. So great was his showmanship that people clamored to see the famous fakes. His most notorious fake was the Feejee Mermaid, a creature that was a combination of a monkey and a fish, but was actually half a monkey sewn to half a fish!

#TENWORDS

BILLY BEANE

"We must find value in things that others can't see".

Inspired by Billy Beane's ability to get his low budget Oakland A's to beat much richer teams, I encouraged small brands to compete with much richer ones when I was at Facebook. Considering how *organic* growth is driven by great content and not just great budgets, I told brands that social media was the one area of business where they didn't need to outspend their competitors in order to beat them. This is still true today.

READ: *Moneyball* (Book by Michael Lewis)
WATCH: *Moneyball* (Screenplay by Aaron Sorkin)
FOLLOW: @athletics

Business is an unfair game. Brands and organisations compete against each other for market share, mind share and customer attention and it is usually the business with the deepest pockets that wins. In 2002, American baseball team the Oakland A's were trying to compete against the New York Yankee's. The A's had a budget of $39 million for their team. The Yankee's had almost three times that ($114 million). Immortalised in the 2011 film *Moneyball*, Brad Pitt played Billy Beane as the general manager who was forced to find a different way to compete. There was no way they were going to be able to outspend the Yankee's or afford to compete for the leagues best players, so they had to find ways to think differently. In order to compete with the Yankee's *on* the field, Beane knew that his Oakland A's had to act differently *off* the field.

Moneyball was the term applied to Billy Beane's concept of baseball economics where he pioneered the use of technology to predict player performance. He used computer algorithms to find hidden value in data that other's couldn't see, in order to compete with the richer teams. Players with quirky playing styles for example, may have been written off by other teams, but data might show that those players could be used differently to form a winning team. It worked. In 2002 the Athletics became the first team in 100 years of American League baseball to win 20 consecutive games.

#**TEN**WORDS

BILLY BEANE

MONEYBALL
BRAD PITT   JONAH HILL   PHILIP SEYMOUR HOFFMAN

#**TEN**WORDS

PETER BENENSON

"Better to light a candle than to curse the darkness".

Amnesty International has 7 million supporters around the world. It was awarded the Nobel Peace Prize in 1977 for its campaign against torture and has issued over 20,500 *"Urgent Actions"* since 1973, by sending millions of letters and short stories sent to world leaders to release *"prisoners of conscience"* who are in immediate danger.

READ: *Keepers of the Flame* by Stephen Hopgood
WATCH: Amnesty International's YouTube Channel
FOLLOW: @Amnesty

On the 28th May in 1961, a British lawyer and former World War II codebreaker called Peter Benenson wrote a story which would change the future of human rights forever. The story titled *"The Forgotten Prisoners"* was published in The Observer newspaper and was an instant sensation. Peter wrote provocatively about the *Universal Declaration of Human Rights* after hearing that two Portuguese students were imprisoned for raising a toast to freedom. The article was reprinted in newspapers across the world and provoked a flood of responses from readers who challenged their governments to look closer at human rights abuses. Peter called for an *"Appeal for Amnesty"* and Amnesty International was born, forming a human rights organisation which would campaign for *"freedom"* in 150 countries. Who says a short story can't inspire a small group of people to take action and change the world? The pen is indeed mightier than the sword. From the age of 14, I was on one of Amnesty's *"Urgent Action"* teams. Before the days of the internet, I waited to receive the Amnesty newsletter by mail every Tuesday at 8:30am, with a list of human rights violations and the names and addresses of minsters who I could write to. I could never be sure that my two sentence letters to the leaders of countries such as Myanmar, Libya and Egypt would make a difference, but at least I felt like I was doing *something*. I loved feeling part of something much bigger than myself. Thanks Peter.

#TENWORDS

"Never doubt that a small group of thoughtful, committed citizens can change the world; indeed, it's the only thing that ever has„.

MARGARET MEAD

#TENWORDS

MARC BENIOFF

"Companies don't compete against each other, they compete against *speed*".

Marc Benioff interned under Steve Jobs at Apple as an assembly language programmer on the Mac team, but it was Oracle where he received his apprenticeship. After 13 years he became Larry Ellison's right hand man and Oracle's youngest ever VP, before leaving to compete against his mentor with a new CRM platform that he developed with Salesforce co-founder Parker Harris.

READ: *Behind the Cloud* by Marc Benioff
WATCH: Benioff interviews from Davos
FOLLOW: @Benioff | $CRM

Most people join a new company for the package. Some move because they like the product or work place. I moved to Salesforce because I liked the person leading the company. It's easy to be impressed by Marc Benioff. You may have seen him at Dreamforce or read about his pioneering approach to cloud computing or 'Software as a Service' (years before everyone else realised it was productive *and* profitable). More recently you might have been impressed by his campaigning for LBGT and women's rights, but what impressed me the most was the corporate (1:1:1) and employee (V2MOM) models which Benioff created. The 1:1:1 model (adopted by Dropbox, Google and GoPro) means committing to giving 1% of product, 1% of equity and 1% of employee's time to charitable causes each year. To date, Salesforce has given free software to over 25,000 non-profit organisations, donated over $100M in grants and given over 1M hours of voluntary service. Employees are willing to do this because it is built into their V2MOM, something Benioff created with the help of Tony Robbins. Short for *vision, values, methods, obstacles* and *methods*, the V2MOM is a personal business plan and mission statement which every employee completes annually every February. It is these models which inspire employees to compete and work faster. Why? Because they don't just feel like they are working for a company, they are working for a *cause*.

#**TEN**WORDS

MARC BENIOFF

Marc Benioff and Tony Robbins with the first V2MOM that they wrote on the back of an AMEX envelope to found Salesforce in 1999.

Salesforce.com's First V2MOM, 4/12/1999

Vision

Rapidly create a world-class Internet company/site for sales Force Automation.

Values

1. World-class organization
2. Time to market
3. Functional
4. Usability (Amazon quality)
5. Value-added partnerships

Methods

1. Hire the team
2. Finalize product specification and technical architecture
3. Rapidly develop the product specification to beta and production stages
4. Build partnerships with big e-commerce, content, and hosting companies
5. Build a launch plan
6. Develop exit strategy: IPO/acquisition

Obstacles

1. Developers
2. Product manager/business development person

Measures

1. Prototype is state-of-the-art
2. High-quality functional system
3. Partnerships are online and integrated
4. Salesforce.com is regarded as leader and visionary
5. We are all rich

#**TEN**WORDS

Sir TIM BERNERS-LEE

"If people are more connected they might not shoot each other".

Sir Tim credits his status as *"inventor of the World Wide Web"* to random chance. *"I happened to be in the right place at the right time, and I happened to have the right combination of background,"* Berners-Lee once said of the reasons he wrote the proposal, which he made while working at Switzerland's CERN nuclear research facility and trying to connect the organization's resources.

READ: *Weaving the Web* by Tim Berners-Lee
WATCH: Sir Tim's interview at Le Web in 2014
FOLLOW: @TimBerners_Lee

I first met Sir Tim Berners-Lee at the tech conference SXSW in 2012 where I was due to interview him for a book I was working on. I couldn't have been more excited to see him, so I was devastated when I found out at the last minute that his PR's changed their mind and refused my request to spend 12 minutes with him. All I wanted was a quote about his legacy. Instead, I was informed that Sir Tim had only ever given one quote for a book, and that was to Al Gore. Fair enough I thought, but it still seemed slightly bizarre that the man who *"invented"* the world wide web and *"gave"* it to the world *for free*, wouldn't give me a quote to inspire young marketers. Luckily, marketing magazine *The Drum* asked Sir Tim the same question that I wanted to. His response was a good one. So good in fact that I shall re-print it here and pretend he gave it to me first...

"Hopefully the web will make the human race work more efficiently: we've already seen acceleration of commerce, and the acceleration of learning. The big question is can we use it to accelerate peace? One of the worrying things when people go online is that they tend to interact with their own kind: race, colour, creed, sexual preference and so on. People tend to stick to their own on the web. So the big thing is to get people to connect across cultural borders. If you've just been in conversation with somebody about some common interest you are less likely to shoot them."

#**TEN**WORDS

Sir TIM BERNERS-LEE

CERN DD/OC
Information Management: A Proposal

Tim Berners-Lee, CERN/DD
March 1989

Information Management: A Proposal

Abstract

This proposal concerns the management of general information about accelerators and experiments at CERN. It discusses the problems of loss of information about complex evolving systems and derives a solution based on a distributed hypertext sytstem.

Keywords: Hypertext, Computer conferencing, Document retrieval, Information management, Project control

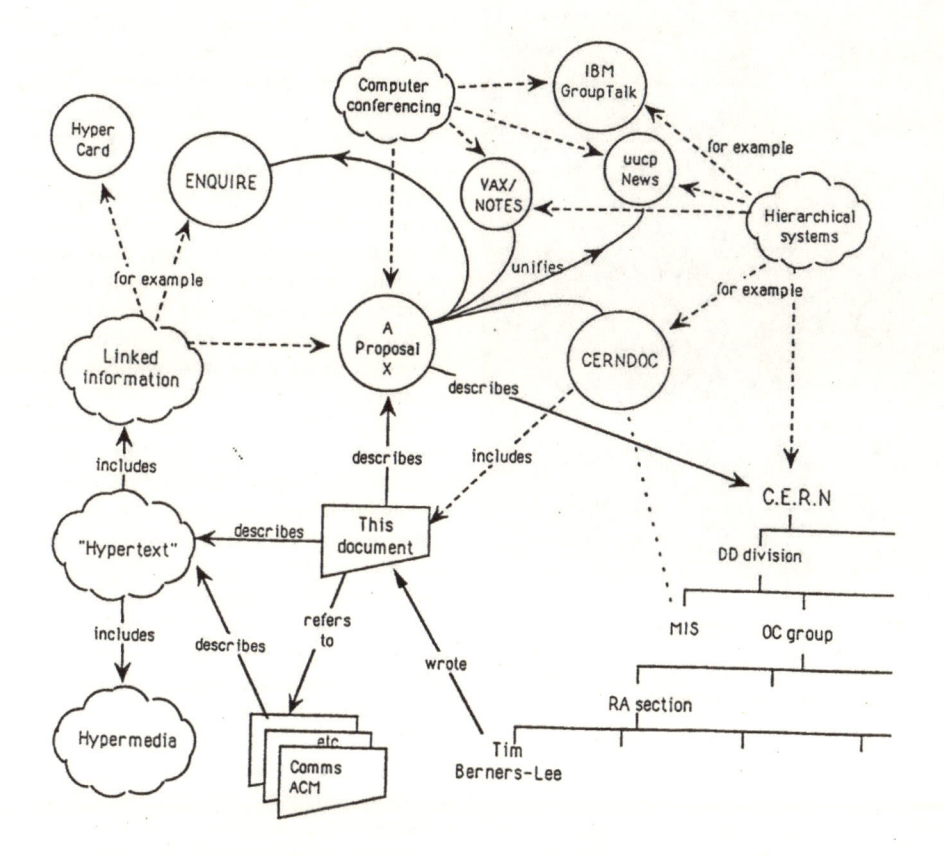

Sir Tim Berners-Lee's original diagram explaining how his concept of a *'world wide web'* might work. His line manager would later write on the top of the paper *"Vague but exciting"*.

#TENWORDS

JEFF BEZOS

"Life is too short to hang out with un-resourceful people".

Jeff Bezos has a *'Two Pizza Rule'* to makes sure that all the teams across Amazon stay agile and remain competitive. It is a philosophy he has instilled in his managers and the reason why Amazon teams usually consist of less than ten people: *"If you can't feed your team with two large pizzas, your team is too big"*.

READ: *The Everything Store* by Brad Stone
WATCH: Jeff Bezos at Code Conference 2016
FOLLOW: @JeffBezos | $AMZN

Amazon.com is one of the most extraordinary companies in business today. Amazon CEO and founder Jeff Bezos (on paper the richest person in the world) has always found a way to capitalise on technology trends, whether being an early online retailer, seeing the future of cloud computing and forming Amazon Web Services or developing delivery drones and commercial rockets. *"We've built stuff nobody has built before with development process and methodologies that didn't exist"* Bezos has said. In the early days when Amazon started AWS, cynical journalists wondered who would want to buy storage from a book shop (just like Borders originally suggested that a book store without stores wouldn't succeed). Since the very beginning Amazon has relied on several key building blocks and the *'Flywheel Effect'* to maintain its technology edge. *The Flywheel Effect* is the idea that once you have your core tech pieces in place, they have an energy of their own that drives other positive changes and innovations. *The Flywheel* had very humble beginnings, first appearing on the back of a napkin after a brainstorming workshop with Jeff's leadership team. The team were trying to articulate Amazon's growth strategy for the future, when Bezos simply drew 10 words around the word *"growth"*. It is this beautifully simple idea that has driven Amazon's success since it's IPO in 1997. Twenty years later, Amazon is now the 10th largest brand on the planet.

#**TEN**WORDS

JEFF BEZOS

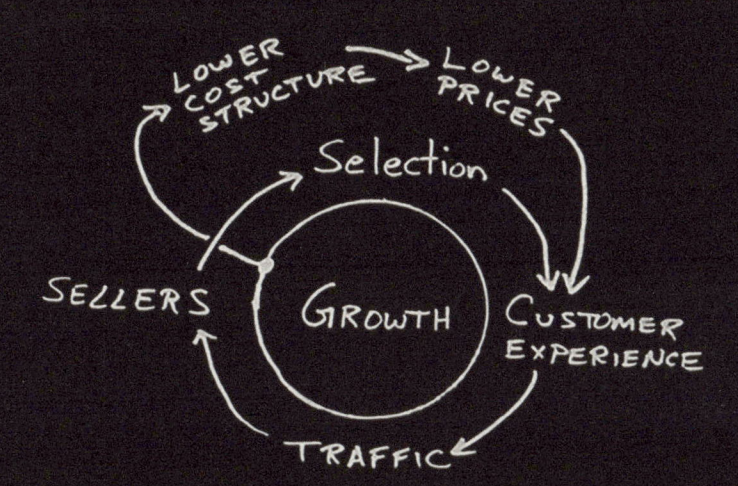

[Diagram: Hand-drawn flywheel with "GROWTH" at the center, surrounded by "Selection", "Customer Experience", "Traffic", "Sellers", leading to "Lower Cost Structure" and "Lower Prices"]

AMAZON'S *"FLYWHEEL EFFECT"*

Jeff Bezos and his lieutenants sketched their own virtuous cycle, which they believe powered their business. It went something like this: Lower prices led to more customer visits. More customers increased the volume of sales and attracted more commission-paying third party sellers to the site. That allowed Amazon to get more out of fixed costs like the fulfillment centers and the servers they needed to run the website. This greater efficiency then enabled it to lower prices further. Feed any part of this flywheel… and it should accelerate the loop. Amazon executives were elated when they first saw it… after five years, they felt like they finally understood their business.

The ten words written around the word "Growth" continue to drive Amazon's strategy today, proving that the best strategies can always be written on the back of a napkin.

#TENWORDS

MICHAEL BLOOMBERG

"Be the first one in and the last one out".

"Life is too short to spend your time avoiding failure". Another ten words of advice from the ex-Mayor of New York.

READ: *Bloomberg* By Bloomberg
WATCH: BloombergTV
FOLLOW: @Technology

Michael Bloomberg is a businessman, author, politician, and philanthropist worth around US$50 billion. I love him because he built the one TV channel I watch everyday, Bloomberg Technology. Unlike *"other"* New Yorker's who have made successful runs for political office (he was the mayor of New York), Bloomberg's fortune was self made. So what advice does he give to any budding entrepreneur or politician wishing to follow in his footsteps? Just ten words…
"Be the first one in and the last one out".

This philosophy has nothing to do with his work ethic as you might expect, it was simply the best way to meet important people. Secretaries and 'gate keepers' he discovered, didn't arrive until 8am, so the best executives often answered their own phone if you called them early enough. When Michael was first building Bloomberg, he'd go to the deli across the street from Merrill Lynch's headquarters at 6am and buy coffee (with and without milk) and tea (with and without milk), plus a few sugars on the side. He'd then roam the halls to see if anyone was sat alone in their office with a newspaper. If they were he'd walk in and say, *"Hi, I'm Mike Bloomberg. I brought you a coffee. I'd just like to bend your ear"*. Nobody says *"Go away!"* to the guy who brought them tea or coffee. It was a ridiculously simple idea, but one that helped Mike to build some of the most influential relationships on Wall Street.

#TENWORDS

THE FUTURE NEEDS A BIG KISS

(AND SO DO YOU)

#TENWORDS

BONO

"Feelings are stronger than ideas or words in a song".

Bono receives a lot of critisism for his political activism, but few people realise the impact that his campaigning has achieved. In 2006 he founded (RED) with Bobby Shriver of the ONE Campaign. To date (RED) has raised over $465 million to help eliminate AIDS/HIV in 8 African countries, through partnerships with Apple, Nike, AMEX, Starbucks, Coke and GAP.

READ: *Bono on Bono* by Michka Assayas
WATCH: Bono's TED Talk: *The Good News on Poverty*
FOLLOW: @U2 | @RED

I love U2. They were my favourite band growing up, so I was overjoyed to find myself on the front row at Web Summit in Dublin a few years ago when Bono was speaking. He was there to talk about technology and serious things, but I loved how animated he became when he started to talk about his song writing process.

"You can have 1,000 ideas, but unless you capture an emotion, it's an essay. I'm always writing speeches or articles for causes I believe in. That's probably what I would have done if I wasn't in music, but that's not songwriting. Songwriting comes from a different place. Music is the language of the spirit. I think ideas and words are our excuse as songwriters to allow our heart or our spirit to run free. That's when magic happens."

It is only after U2 find that powerful emotion upon which they can hang some words off that Bono begins to write the lyrics. Sometimes he'll draw phrases or lines from the notebook he carries with him, but he usually just tries to capture the spontaneous feeling the music inspires in him - a creative strategy he learned listening to Lennon's first two solo albums, *Plastic Ono and Imagine*. The Web Summit interview was great, even better than I expected, but what I loved best was when Bono was asked to describe himself. And that he did, in (you guessed it!) ten words: *"I'm a scribbling, smoking, wine drinking, Bible reading band man"*.

BONO

THE (RED)™ MANIFESTO

ALL THINGS BEING EQUAL, THEY ARE NOT.

AS FIRST WORLD CONSUMERS, WE HAVE TREMENDOUS POWER. WHAT WE COLLECTIVELY CHOOSE TO BUY, OR NOT TO BUY, CAN CHANGE THE COURSE OF LIFE AND HISTORY ON THIS PLANET.

(RED) IS THAT SIMPLE AN IDEA. AND THAT POWERFUL. NOW, YOU HAVE A CHOICE. THERE ARE (RED) CREDIT CARDS, (RED) PHONES, (RED) SHOES, (RED) FASHION BRANDS. AND NO, THIS DOES NOT MEAN THEY ARE ALL RED IN COLOR, ALTHOUGH SOME ARE.

IF YOU BUY A (RED) PRODUCT OR SIGN UP FOR A (RED) SERVICE, AT NO COST TO YOU, A (RED) COMPANY WILL GIVE SOME OF ITS PROFITS TO BUY AND DISTRIBUTE ANTI-RETROVIRAL MEDICINE TO OUR BROTHERS AND SISTERS DYING OF AIDS IN AFRICA.

WE BELIEVE THAT WHEN CONSUMERS ARE OFFERED THIS CHOICE, AND THE PRODUCTS MEET THEIR NEEDS, THEY WILL CHOOSE (RED). AND WHEN THEY CHOOSE (RED) OVER NON-(RED), THEN MORE BRANDS WILL CHOOSE TO BECOME (RED) BECAUSE IT WILL MAKE GOOD BUSINESS SENSE TO DO SO. AND MORE LIVES WILL BE SAVED.

(RED) IS NOT A CHARITY. IT IS SIMPLY A BUSINESS MODEL. YOU BUY (RED) STUFF, WE GET THE MONEY, BUY THE PILLS AND DISTRIBUTE THEM. THEY TAKE THE PILLS, STAY ALIVE, AND CONTINUE TO TAKE CARE OF THEIR FAMILIES AND CONTRIBUTE SOCIALLY AND ECONOMICALLY IN THEIR COMMUNITIES.

IF THEY DON'T GET THE PILLS, THEY DIE. WE DON'T WANT THEM TO DIE. WE WANT TO GIVE THEM THE PILLS. AND WE CAN. AND YOU CAN. AND IT'S EASY.

ALL YOU HAVE TO DO IS UPGRADE YOUR CHOICE.

#TENWORDS

Sir DAVE BRAILSFORD

"There's no 'I' in team. But there is a 'me'".

In 2004 the British cycling team won their first two gold medals in 100 years, but then Brailsford took over. Over the following decade TeamGB led the cycling medal table at the 2008 and 2012 Olympic Games and won 59 World Championships across different disciplines between 2003-2013.

READ: Brailsford's 20 Lessons in Leadership
WATCH: Brailsford's Keynote at Institute of Directors
FOLLOW: @TeamSky | @TeamGB

Sir Dave Brailsford is credited with championing the philosophy of *'marginal gains'* at British Cycling. The concept comes from the idea that if you broke down everything you could think of that goes into riding a bike, and then improved it by 1%, you would get a significant increase when you put them all together. In 2010, Brailsford became the manager of the new British-based professional team, Team Sky. Sir Dave's vision for the team was to win one Tour de France within 5 years. He failed. He won FOUR. In 2017 he won Team Sky's fifth.

How did he become so successful? I was eager to find out so I arranged for us to have a coffee so I could ask him. The answer was quite simple. He didn't worry about egos or emotions and instead focused purely on vision and purpose. Elite athletes are divas. They have big egos, large followings and lucrative endorsement deals. And many of them don't get on with each other. *"There is no 'I' in team"* Brailsford told me, *"but there are lots of 'me's"*, so instead of worrying about creating a happy team culture where everyone got on, he only concentrated on making sure that every athlete was focused on exactly the same team goal. In this case, winning the Tour de France. *"Organisations worry to much about harmony"*, he told me. *"Happy teams often don't win. As long as everyone is focused on the same goal, I don't really care whether they get on with each other or not"*.

#TENWORDS

Sir RICHARD BRANSON

"You should judge me by the quality of my children".

Sir Richard Branson is one of the world's most respected entrepreneurs and an inspiration to business leaders everywhere. This is not just because of his wealth and commercial success, but because of the way that he has fought against his dyslexia and a poor academic performance (he dropped out of school soon after his sixteenth birthday). A campaigner for people with dyslexia, Sir Richard said, "People should think about dyslexia differently in order to combat the stigma around it. they should recognise all of the great people who struggled with dyslexia. At school my dyslexia was treated as a handicap. My teachers thought I was lazy and dumb, and I couldn't keep up or fit in". That feeling became the fuel which drove him to be successful in business.

"The reason why I think people who are dyslexic seem to do well in life, having struggled at school, is that we tend to simplify things". It is this simplicity that I admire most about Sir Richard. He is driven by a desire to succeed, not just a desire to make more money. Unlike many entrepreneurs, he values the *quality* of his life more than *quantity* of his empire. Simon Sinek shared with me a conversation he had with Sir Richard in early 2017. Instead of asking him about his *"why"* as Sinek often does, Sinek asked him, *"When you're gone, how do you want people to judge you?"*. Without even a seconds hesitation, Branson responded with these ten words.

Branson is one of the UK's richest people with a net worth of over £4.5Bn. He built his Virgin empire, which comprises 400 companies, from the age of 16, doing everything from mobiles to banking to aviation and he's trying to give Elon Musk a run for his money on space travel. I love that one of his habits is never going anywhere without his notebook and a nice pen.

READ: *Screw It, Let's Do It* by Sir Richard Branson
WATCH: *Don't Look Down*, by Daniel Gordon
FOLLOW: @RichardBranson

#TENWORDS

BRENÉ BROWN

"Connection is what gives purpose and meaning to our lives".

Brené Brown is a research professor at the University of Houston Graduate College of Social Work. Like many memorable and inspirational leaders, she has chosen to focus her career on just one small area, by dedicating her time to studying the emotions of *vulnerability, courage, authenticity,* and *shame*.

READ: *Rising Strong* by Brené Brown
WATCH: *The Power of Vulnerability* TED Talk
FOLLOW: @BreneBrown

Brené Brown is a woman who loves her work. She is an outstanding storyteller but hates being referred to as one. She thinks it undermines her stature as a research professor, but in the opening to her wildly popular TEDx talk, she concedes that she probably is one. *"I'm a qualitative researcher. I collect stories… and maybe stories are just data with a soul"*.

Stories are just data with a soul.

I love that line. And I love that she values her work so deeply and works on her research so passionately that it impacts her life. How many other researchers do you know who would claim that their work changed the way that they *lived, loved, worked* and *parented*? Those words, taken from the TEDx talk she gave in Texas back in 2010, have travelled far since then. Shortly after giving her presentation Brené told her friend how embarrassed she was that she'd opened up like that and how terrified she was that the talk would be put online where *"up to 500 people might see it. Or, imagine, a thousand. My life would be over,"* she said. But a few more than that did – the video exploded and now more than 29 million people have watched it. Despite her popularity, Brené hates the spotlight which just makes me like her even more. *"I don't like the cult of personality celebrity stuff. It should be about the work, right? I'm not that interesting. The work is really interesting "*. Bravo.

#**TEN**WORDS

THOMAS BURBERRY

"There's no such thing as bad weather just bad clothing".

The Burberry Equestrian Knight Logo was developed in 1901 and contains the Latin word "*Prorsum*", meaning forwards. Never was a motto more appropriate than when it was woven into Burberry coats which were adapted for soldiers during World War I. And so the *"trench coat"* was born.

Many people mistake entrepreneurs for risk takers. They're not. Entrepreneurs are problem solvers. You are probably familiar with Burberry the fashion brand and their iconic checks, but you may be less familiar with the part they played in some of the world's most historical events. In the late 1800's drapers couldn't see the commercial potential in creating a lightweight, breathable and waterproof fabric, but Thomas Burberry had a different view. Recognised by his friends for *"seeing the world differently"* Thomas became obsessed with creating this innovative fabric that could cope with any weather but remained comfortable and un-restrictive. By finding a new way to waterproof yarn before it was woven, Thomas invented *"the garbadine"*. Over the next few years, this innovative material helped to inspire people to do things that were previously deemed impossible. In 1911 Burberry became the outfitters for Roald Amundsen, the first man to reach the South Pole and Ernest Shackleton, who led a 1914 expedition to cross Antarctica, but my favourite story is a little more quaint. When aviator Betty Kirby-Green wanted to break the world record for the fastest return flight from London to Cape Town in 1937, she was unable to fund the trip. Keen to help her write her name in the history books, Burberry not only designed her jacket, but funded the trip by sponsoring their plane. *"The Burberry"* broke the record and brought Betty home in 45 hours.

READ: *Shackleton's Incredible Voyage* by A. Lansing
WATCH: The Tale of Thomas Burberry
FOLLOW: @Burberry

#**TEN**WORDS

ANDREW CARNEGIE

"Concentration is my motto – first honesty, then industry, then concentration".

Carnegie once wrote that *"the man who dies rich dies disgraced"*. His philosophy was simple. He encouraged people to spend the first third of one's life getting all the education one can, to then spend the next third making all the money one can, and finally to spend the last third giving it all away for worthwhile causes.

READ: *Andrew Carnegie* by David Nasaw
WATCH: *Andrew Carnegie: Prince of Steel*
FOLLOW: His example.

If I could build anything I wanted to, I would probably build a library because I love books so much. Andrew Carnegie loved books too, but he did more than build a library. He built 2,500 of them. And he didn't just build them to help people learn. He wanted to make a statement. When asked what that statement was, his response was swift: *"The older I get the less I listen to what people say and the more I look at what they do"*.

Born in Scotland in 1835, Andrew Carnegie built a steel empire and amassed a personal fortune in excess of $309 billion. He was arguably the greatest businessman and social entrepreneur who ever lived, who had a complex character full of contradictions. He supported workers' rights but destroyed unions. He believed in corporate battles but paid somebody to fight in the American Civil War for him. He acquired one of the largest fortunes in the world and tried to give it all away. He was one of the most inspirational and effective philanthropists who ever lived, but he didn't believe in giving handouts to the poor. *"The great successes of life are made by concentration"*, Carnegie used to tell his employees. *"Do not make riches, but usefulness, your first aim; and let your chief pride be that your daily occupation is in the line of progress and development; that your work, in whatever capacity it may be, is useful work, honestly conducted, and as such ennobling to your life"*. Great advice as relevant today as it was over 100 years ago.

#TENWORDS

ANDREW CARNEGIE

Carnegie Free Library, Charlotte, N. C.

#TENWORDS

DALE CARNEGIE

"Talk to someone about themselves and they'll listen for hours".

"You can make more friends in two months by becoming interested in other people than you can in two years by trying to get other people interested in you". Dale Carnegie*

READ: How To Win Friends And Influence People
WATCH: Dale Carnegie: A Man of Influence
FOLLOW: @DaleCarnegie

Dale Carnegie is best known for penning the 1936 classic *How to Win Friends and Influence People*, but I think it is his later book *Public Speaking: Influencing Men in Business* which is his real masterpiece. Carnegie was a showman, but a humble one. He felt called to inspire others to be better and wanted to reach as many people as possible with his message. By the time he wrote *Public Speaking* in 1945, he had already taught tens of thousands of people.

It all started when Dale risked his money on an expensive ad in the New York Times, inviting businessmen to a seminar on public speaking in 1916. Although not related to Andrew Carnegie, a famous business magnate and philanthropist at the time, Dale rented New York's Carnegie Hall to give his lecture. Dale was worried that no one would turn up, but he under-estimated New York's appetite for professional storytellers. To a packed hall, Dale taught presentation skills, confidence, speech, language, timing, delivery and diction. Each session ended with a challenge. Business leaders had to give their own pitch, but because attention spans were so short (in 1916), Carnegie insisted that pitches lasted no longer than 75 seconds! I'll never forget presenting at a Google conference in 2016 for B2B brands and hearing Google's advice to all content creators? Make sure that your videos are no longer than 75 seconds! The more things change the more they stay the same...

* Dale Carnegie was originally 'Carnegey' but he changed the spelling of his surname so that people might associate him with Andrew Carnegie.

#TENWORDS

DALE CARNEGIE

*** PUBLIC SPEAKING MANIFESTO ***

"Do not sit down and try to manufacture a speech in thirty minutes. A speech can't be cooked to order like a steak. A speech must grow. Select your topic early in the week, think it over during odd moments, brood over it, sleep over it, dream over it. Discuss it with your friends. Make it a topic of conversation. Ask yourself all possible questions concerning it.

Put down on pieces of paper all thoughts and illustrations that come to you and keep reaching out for more. Idea's, suggestions, illustrations, will come drifting to you at sundry times – when you are bathing, when you are driving down town, when you are waiting for dinner to be served. That was Lincoln's method. It has been the method of almost all successful speakers".

DALE CARNEGIE (1916)

#TENWORDS

COCO CHANEL

"In order to be irreplaceable one must always be different".

"If you're sad, add more lipstick and attack". Coco Chanel

At the age of 17, keen to escape the orphanage in which her parents had abandoned her (aged 12), Gabrielle Chanel turned down the chance to be a seamstress, choosing instead to rebel and become a cabaret singer. It was here, in 1905 at a concert hall called *"La Rotonde"* that she got her nickname *"Coco"*, from the song *Qui qu'a vu Coco*. This was also where she mingled with the rich and famous, a clientele which afforded her the opportunity to sell the hats which she created in her spare time. Coco was clever. She performed for a living but made sure that she was performing for influential business men and investors who could help her achieve her dream of launching a fashion brand. Her hats were well received, (especially by their mistresses!) since they challenged the classical designs of the day. *"I find that women are always over dressed, and never elegant enough"*, Coco complained.

Seeking to right this wrong, she opened a dress shop selling her trademark loose fitting garments which accentuated a woman's natural curves. Unlike the structured dresses that were fashionable at the time, Coco's vision was to focus on how women *felt* when they wore the clothes, not how they might appeal to men. It was this simple but unique perspective which challenged the status quo and won her the affection of confident independent women everywhere who wanted to think (and dress) differently.

READ: Vogue on Chanel
WATCH: *No. 5*, Baz Lurhmann's epic $18M Chanel Ad
FOLLOW: @Chanel

#TENWORDS

COCO CHANEL

Madame Gabrielle Chanel in her new apartment in the Ritz, Paris

Photo by Kollar, courtesy Harper's Bazaar

Madame Gabrielle Chanel is above all an artist in living. Her dresses, her perfumes, are created with a faultless instinct for drama. Her Perfume No. 5 is like the soft music that underlies the playing of a love scene. It kindles the imagination; indelibly fixes the scene in the memories of the players.

LES PARFUMS

CHANEL

GLAMOUR de CHANEL   GARDENIA de CHANEL   CUIR de RUSSIE (Russia Leather)

No.5 CHANEL

CHANEL Print Ad *(1937)*

#**TEN**WORDS

YVON CHOUINARD

"When everything goes wrong – that's when the adventure really starts".

"Businesses need profits to survive. The less we make, the less we will have to give away, and the less other companies will think we have a mission that is worth imitating

"How you climb a mountain is more important than reaching the top".

Yvon Chouinard *(Philanthropist and founder of @Patagonia)*

READ: Let My People Go Surfing
WATCH: 180° South
FOLLOW: A map somewhere interesting...

Yvon Chouinard didn't want to be a multi-millionaire businessman, he just wanted to go surfing and climbing. Living out of a camper van for around 250 days a year, Yvon needed to find a way to fund his habit, so he decided to become a tradesman. Training as a blacksmith, Yvon wanted to make "*piton's*" (used by climbers to lock into the cracks of a rock face) because he didn't think the cheaply made European ones which were made from soft iron were good enough. The problem with soft iron pitons is that once they are forced into the rock face, you can't take them out again, which is great for the next climber, but it means that you have to carry a lot of them with you. European piton's were also intended to be left in the rock face for the next group of climbers, enabling even the weakest climbers to make the ascent. Preferring the zen approach of "*leaving a landscape as you found it*", Yvon wanted to make stronger piton's, that may have been ten times the cost but could be used over and over again.

Yvon 's piton's soon gained 80% of the climbing equipment market and allowed Yvon to establish Patagonia, the outdoor brand which makes "*the tools you wear*" and is valued at over $700 million. Yvon remains a passionate environmentalist and founded OnePercentForThePlanet.org which campaigns for brands to use their profits to protect the world around them. It's 1,400 members now fund over 2,000 eco-projects.

#**TEN**WORDS

YVON CHOUINARD

DON'T BUY THIS JACKET

COMMON THREADS INITIATIVE

REDUCE
WE make useful gear that lasts a long time
YOU don't buy what you don't need

REPAIR
WE help you repair your Patagonia gear
YOU pledge to fix what's broken

REUSE
WE help find a home for Patagonia gear
you no longer need
YOU sell or pass it on*

RECYCLE
WE will take back your Patagonia gear
that is worn out
YOU pledge to keep your stuff out of
the landfill and incinerator

REIMAGINE
TOGETHER we reimagine a world where we take
only what nature can replace

It's Black Friday, the day in the year retail turns from red to black and starts to make real money. But Black Friday, and the culture of consumption it reflects, puts the economy of natural systems that support all life firmly in the red. We're now using the resources of one-and-a-half planets on our one and only planet.

Because Patagonia wants to be in business for a good long time – and leave a world inhabitable for our kids – we want to do the opposite of every other business today. We ask you to buy less and to reflect before you spend a dime on this jacket or anything else.

Environmental bankruptcy, as with corporate bankruptcy, can happen very slowly, then all of a sudden. This is what we face unless we slow down, then reverse the damage. We're running short on fresh water, topsoil, fisheries, wetlands – all our planet's natural systems and resources that support business, and life, including our own.

The environmental cost of everything we make is astonishing. Consider the R2® Jacket shown, one of our best sellers. To make it required 135 liters of water, enough to meet the daily needs (three glasses a day) of 45 people. Its journey from its origin as 60% recycled polyester to our Reno warehouse generated nearly 20 pounds of carbon dioxide, 24 times the weight of the finished product. This jacket left behind, on its way to Reno, two-thirds its weight in waste.

And this is a 60% recycled polyester jacket, knit and sewn to a high standard; it is exceptionally durable, so you won't have to replace it as often. And when it comes to the end of its useful life we'll take it back to recycle into a product of equal value. But, as is true of all the things we can make and you can buy, this jacket comes with an environmental cost higher than its price.

There is much to be done and plenty for us all to do. Don't buy what you don't need. Think twice before you buy anything. Go to patagonia.com/CommonThreads or scan the QR code below. Take the Common Threads Initiative pledge, and join us in the fifth "R," to reimagine a world where we take only what nature can replace.

patagonia
patagonia.com

*If you sell your used Patagonia product on eBay® and take the Common Threads Initiative pledge, we will co-list your product on patagonia.com for no additional charge.

TAKE THE PLEDGE

#TENWORDS

CLAYTON CHRISTENSSEN

"Disruptive technology is a marketing challenge, not a technological one".

Clay Christenssen taught me that *innovation* and *disruption* are two entirely different things. *Innovation* refers to anything that does an existing thing better or faster (*Uber*, *iTunes*), but *disruption* only happens when a new thing comes along and makes the existing thing obsolete (*Amazon.com, Netflix*).

READ: The Innovators DNA by Clay Christenssen
WATCH: How Will You Measure Your Life? TEDxBoston
FOLLOW: @ClayChristenssen

Clayton Christenssen has had a heart attack, a stroke and been diagnosed with cancer. For a Harvard Business professor who has spent his academic life talking about *"disruptive innovation"* (since he was the person who first coined the phrase), it's fair to say that he has had a very disruptive life. Any life changing events such as these cause a person to think differently about their personal and professional life and Clay is no different. But what I love most about Clay is not his superb books or thought-provoking lectures, but the way that he has managed to respectfully weave his faith into business teachings in a way that inspires others.

*"Innovators **need** a heavy dose of faith"*, Clay says. *"They need to trust their intuition that they are working on a big idea. But that faith need not be blind. **You must decide what you stand for. And then stand for it all the time**"*. The mistake that most business people make, Clay argues, is that they should either have faith in science *or* religion. They wrongly believe that they can't have both. What they should be doing, is searching for *truth*. Sometimes the answer may be *spiritual*. Sometimes it may be *scientific*. But if you constantly search for truth, you are never going to be *"disrupted"* by an argument which appears contrary to your beliefs. Asking the right questions, Clay once told me, is far more important than believing you have the right answers. More business leaders need to have faith (in something).

#TENWORDS

CLAYTON CHRISTENSSEN

THE 3 P'S OF THE WORLD'S MOST INNOVATIVE COMPANIES

People

- Senior executive(s) lead the innovative charge and excel at "discovery".
- Monitor and maintain an adequate proportion of adventurous and discovery driven people in every management level, functional area, and decision-making stage of the innovation process.
- Hire problem solvers over risk takers.

Processes

- Processes explicitly encourage employees to associate, question, observe, network and experiment.
- Processes are designed to hire, train, enable, reward, and promote discovery-driven people.
- Every person is able to describe what they do as a simple process.

Philosophies

1. Innovation is everyone's job – not just R&D.
2. Create cultures where disruption is encouraged.
3. Deploy small, properly organised innovation project teams consisting of subject matter experts who encourage *"design thinking"*.
4. Take smart risks in pursuit of innovation.

@CLAYCHRISTENSEEN

"You can talk all you want about having a clear purpose and strategy for your life, but ultimately this means nothing if you are not investing the resources you have in a way that is consistent with your strategy. In the end, a strategy is nothing but good intentions unless it's effectively implemented".

#TENWORDS

Sir WINSTON CHURCHILL

"All great things can be expressed in a single word".

[FREEDOM. JUSTICE. HONOR. DUTY. MERCY. HOPE. LOVE]

"A good speech should be like a woman's skirt; long enough to cover the subject and short enough to create interest".

Winston Churchill

READ: *My Early Life* by Winston Churchill
WATCH: "*Their Finest Hour*" Speech (June 18, 1940).
FOLLOW: @ChurchillQuote

The average person's vocabulary contains around 25,000 words. Churchill's has been estimated at 65,000. He loved words and understood the power of rhetoric, able to perfectly place small words within short powerful sentences which resonated deeply with his audiences. He once said, "*Of all the talents bestowed upon men, none is so precious as the gift of oratory. He who enjoys it wields a power more durable than that of a great king*".

Much has been written about Churchill's words and achievements, but little has been written about his communication techniques. As a young man, Winston's ambition was the be a "*master of the spoken word*", something that he achieved through constant practice. He obsessed over every word and even went as far as visualising every speech in advance, anticipating where he was likely to be interrupted so that he would always have a strong response prepared. Churchill despised speakers who were unprepared. He felt like they were neglecting their responsibilities and disrespecting their audience. He promised himself that he would never act like the kind of orator he detested, who "*before they get up, do not know what they are going to say; when they are speaking, do not know what they are saying; and when they have sat down, do not know what they have said*". When Churchill spoke, nobody was in any doubt about what he said or what he meant.

#**TEN**WORDS

Sir WINSTON CHURCHILL

The consummate performer, Churchill would rise, when recognized by the Speaker, with two pairs of glasses in his waistcoat. Perching the long-range pair on the end of his nose at such an angle that he could read his notes while giving the impression that he was looking directly at the House, he gave every appearance of speaking extemporaneously. If the occasion called for quoting a document, he produced his second pair and altered his voice and manner so effectively that even those who knew better believed that everything he said when not quoting was spontaneous.

```
    Upon this battle depends the
        survival of Christian civilization.

    Upon it depends our own British life
        and the long continuity of our
            institutions, and our Empire.

    The whole fury and might of the enemy
        must very soon be turned on us.

    Hitler knows that we will hv to break
        us in this Island, or lose the war.

    If we can stand up to him,
        all Europe may be freed,
            and the life of the world
                may move forward into the
                    broad and sunlit uplands.

    But if we fail,
        then the whole world,
            including the United States,
                and all that we have known and
                                        cared for,
                    will sink into the abyss of a
                        new Dark Age
                            made more sinister and
                                perhaps more prolonged by
                                    the lights of perverted
                                                Science.

    Let us therefore brace ourselves to
        our duty, and so bear ourselves that
            if the British Empire and
                Commonwealth lasts for a
                    thousand years, men will still
                        say,

            'This was their finest hour'.
```

To aid in the flow of delivery, he would set the text of his speeches in what his staff called "psalm form" — a practice that may have been inspired by his love of the Old Testament. To these haiku-esque blocks, he would add notes for their delivery: where to pause and where to expect an ovation; which words and letters to emphasize; even where to appear to stumble a bit, grope for a word, and "correct" himself. Churchill knew that a flawless, robotic recital would put people to sleep and that the more naturalistic a speech seemed, the more tuned in his audience would be.

Churchill had a *"secret side"* concerning how he went about delivering his speeches in Parliament. Once he had the final version of a speech, he typed it on pieces of paper measuring around 4" x 8". The text was set in broken lines (like a Psalm) to aid his delivery, in what he called *"speech form."* It was assumed that these were notes on his topic where in actual fact is was his speech completely written out and delivered word for word.

#TENWORDS

PAULO COELHO

"The world is changed by your example, not your opinion".

"It's not enough to know what you want, you must do what you want in order to be what you want". Paulo Coelho has sold over 200 million books and is the all-time most successful Portuguese author. He averages one book every two years and sees them translated into 80 languages. His most famous book, *The Alchemist*, has sold over 65 million copies worldwide.

READ: Any of his books.
WATCH: Paulo Coelho's *Top 10 Rules For Success*
FOLLOW: @PauloCoelho

Ever since Tim Ferriss introduced me to Paulo Coelho I have been enchanted by his writing (and his love of describing the process of writing). Paulo believes that there are only four different types of stories: a love story between two people, a love story between three people, the struggle for power, and the journey. He contests that every single book in any bookstore deals with one of these four themes, and he uses them as the cornerstones of his own stories.

So if Paulo's formula is so obvious, why does his writing attract such a large and loyal fan base? The answer, as is often the case, is surprisingly simple. He tells big stories, using small words, and leaves as much as possible to the reader's imagination. *"You have to trust your audience"*, he says *"they have a lot of imagination. Don't try to describe things. Give a hint, and they will fulfil this hint with their own imagination"*. This is why Paulo is so reluctant to sell the rights to his books for movies, because they leave nothing to the imagination. He likes his audience to imagine themselves in his world, not have it explained to them in every minor detail. This, Paulo believes, is where most storytellers go wrong, because they underestimate their audience. *"Books are not there to show how intelligent and cultivated you are. Books are out there to show your heart, to show your soul, and to tell your audience: You are not alone"*, he says. That, friends, is why so many people love Paulo.

//#TENWORDS

BRIAN COX

"On TV, things should be made simpler but not simple".

When I was taught thermodynamics at school it took several hours to understand the basics. Brian Cox does it in minutes by building a sandcastle. Brian has a knack for *"reduction"* making enormous subjects seem local and relevant, by subscribing to Einstein's philosophy of communication, *"If you can't explain your physics to a barmaid in a language that she understands, then it's bad physics!*

READ: *Why Does E-mc² ?* (Brian Cox & Jeff Forshaw)
WATCH: *Wonders of the Universe* (BBC TV series)
FOLLOW: @ProfBrianCox

Professor Brian Cox is my favourite modern day scientist. Not because of his work on the Large Hadron Collider at CERN, or the fact he was in a rock band. Neither do I love Brian because he was a superb physics lecturer in my hometown at Manchester University or because we have done a couple of fun gigs together. No, I love Brian because he has the special ability to quickly explain quantum physics to the average person, in a language that they understand, using just a bucket and spade and an umbrella. AND do it in a way that audiences find interesting. Not many people can do that.

It is Brian's unique ability to tell short compelling stories about very complex matters that propelled him from the occasional late night TV appearance or radio interview, to having his own TV primetime show on BBC1. As the face of science for the BBC, Brian has almost single handedly made science for a mass-audience cool in the UK. His passion for science is infectious. And the fact that he loves his work *SO* much and gets genuinely excited about learning new things makes him a very watchable (and successful) TV presenter. He is a master storyteller but he refuses to compromise his scientific integrity by over-simplifying things. Paraphrasing Einstein, Brian's ten word *"Simple Manifesto"* for TV presenting are words which we could all take to heart and learn from. Regardless of whether we'll ever find ourselves in front of a TV camera.

#TENWORDS

MARIE CURIE

"Be less curious about people and more curious about ideas".

Curie believed that people really don't care that much about what you've *done*, they really want to know what you're *doing*. *"Nobody really wants to answer the question, 'What do you do?'..."*, she used to say, *"'What are you working on?" is a much more interesting question"*. Good advice for all of us.

READ: *Madame Curie: A Biography* by Ève Curie
WATCH: *The Genius of Marie Curie*
FOLLOW: *@MarieCurieUK*

In 1911 Marie Curie-Skłodowska became the first woman to win the Noble prize in two different fields (physics and chemistry). She coined the term radioactivity, discovered radium (which eventually killed her), and managed to get things done regardless of the fact that the scientific world didn't always take her seriously. Determined to work harder than everyone else she even declined to attend the Nobel prize ceremony in person because she was *"too busy with her work"*.

Her accomplishments changed how we think about radiation, but she struggled to get the word out because she was a woman. Refusing to be bitter about the way that she was treated publicly, she rose above the criticism by going out of her way to be generous which included offering up her radium-isolation process patent-free so others could continue her research. To the ego-obsessed scientists of the day, this kind of thinking was revolutionary which only added to her appeal. Curie was the subject of all kinds of *"table-talk"*, but when journalists or writers would ask her about gossip or secrets, Curie would respond with just ten words, *"Be less curious about people and more curious about ideas"*. Curie hated that people focused on her sex, and not her accomplishments. Her point was simple: if people struggle to separate you from what you do, then your work isn't speaking for itself.

#TENWORDS

MARIE CURIE

"Humanity surely needs practical men who make the best of their work for the sake of their own interests, without forgetting the general interest.

But it also needs DREAMERS, for whom the unselfish following of a purpose is so imperative that it becomes impossible for them to devote much attention to their own material benefit."

MARIE SKLOWDOWSKA CURIE

#TENWORDS

MILES DAVIS

"It takes you a long time to sound like yourself".

When Miles was at Julliard School in New York, some of the cities most famous jazz artists turned up the play at lunch and inspire the students. The artists couldn't understand why few students ever turned up, until they realised that every practice room was always booked up. Eager to create the future instead of learning from the past, Miles recalled later that he practiced hard because of his ten word philosophy, *"It takes you a long time to sound like yourself"*.

READ: *Miles* by Miles Davis
WATCH: *Miles Ahead* with Don Cheadle
FOLLOW: @BlueNoteRecords

Jazz trumpeter and composer Miles Dewey Davis III was not what you would call a humble man. The multi-talented musician attempted to make it easier for one journalist seeking to describe his career by telling them that he "*changed music five or six times.*" He wasn't joking. Davis was inducted into the Rock and Roll Hall of Fame in 2006 for being "*one of the key figures in the history of jazz*". His album *Kind of Blue* is the greatest jazz album ever recorded.

"It's not the note you play that's the wrong note - it's the note you play afterwards that makes it right or wrong".

Miles started his career when he left Julliard School in New York because he was bored of playing two-note 'bop-bop' every 90 bars in the symphony, so he left. He thought the school was too *"white-oriented"*. One example was when a white female teacher told his class the reason black people played the blues was because they were poor and had to pick cotton. Davis wrote that he raised his hand, stood up, and said, "*I'm from East St. Louis and my father is rich, he's a dentist, and I play the blues. My father didn't never pick no cotton and I didn't wake up this morning sad and start playing the blues. There's more to it than that.*" From that moment Miles was driven by a deep desire to prove himself and make his mark on the music industry by playing the kind of jazz that nobody expected to hear.

#TENWORDS

ROBERT DE NIRO

"You can tell a whole story in six seconds". [Robert De Niro only needs 9 words]

Robert De Niro has the power to captivate an audience in seconds whether on the screen or on the page. He is a big fan of short stories and an admirer of movie mogul Samuel Goldwyn who once said, *"If you can't write your movie idea on the back of a business card you ain't got a movie!"*

READ: *"The Shadow King"*. Vanity Fair (2014)
WATCH: Taxi
FOLLOW: De Niro's example: Write short. Speak fast.

Writing a long story is quite easy. Writing a short story is hard. It's hard enough writing a good screenplay that lasts minutes or hours, but what about one that only lasts a few seconds? That was the challenge facing brands in early 2013 when the (ill-fated) six-second looping video app Vine launched. At the time, I was working for Adobe on social strategy and was asked for my thoughts about the new service for some PR comments. I quickly wrote an opinion piece of around 1,000 carefully crafted words about attention spans, millennials and the changing nature of storytelling. I covered the pros and cons of Vine and contemplated how it might impact the future of advertising and branded content. It was a great piece but not one word of it was printed. Why? Because when Robert De Niro turned up at a premier he was attending in London, he was asked about Vine. The second he opened his mouth, he instantly stole my column inches.

"Six seconds of beginning, middle and end. I was just trying to time on my iPhone six seconds just to get a sense of what that is. It can actually be a long time. One one-thousand, two one-thousand, three one-thousand, four one-thousand, five one-thousand, six one-thousand - you can tell a whole story in six seconds."

I completely missed the brevity that this situation required. A comment on short-form video did not require 1,000 words. It only required nine. So De Niro's nine words became the headline. Well played Taxi man.

> If you can't write your idea on the back of a business card, you ain't got a movie.
>
> SAMUEL GOLDWYN

#**TEN**WORDS

W. EDWARDS DEMING

"Innovation comes from those who take joy in their work".

Deming was an American statistician and consultant whose advocacy of quality-control methods in industrial production aided Japan's economic recovery after World War II. His processes are responsible for spurring the global success of many Japanese brands such as Honda and Toyota. He was famous for challenging quality control and supply chain managers, *"If you can't describe what you do as a process, you don't know what you're doing"*.

READ: Out of Crisis by W. Edwards Deming
WATCH: "Deming 14 Points"
FOLLOW: Blog.Deming.Org

I first heard these ten words during a conversation with Carlos Ghosn, chairman and CEO of the Renault-Nissan Alliance. Carlos was quoting an American statistician by the name of W. Edwards Deming who made a name for himself in the 1960's when he revolutionised the way that quality control was managed in the automobile industry. Carlos told me that while it is important to take joy in your work, enjoying your work doesn't automatically create a culture of *'meaningful innovation'*. *"Innovation is not the same as invention"*, he told me. *"Something is only genuinely innovative if it makes it to market. Innovation is not 'I have invented something'. Nobody cares who invented it. Consumers care about the benefit of the innovation – not who had the idea, but who brought it to market, in marketable conditions"*.

Like Deming, Carlos quotes Thomas Edison as a great example. Edison took great joy in his work, but that's not what made him innovative. As one of the world's most prolific inventors, Edison transitioned from inventor to innovator not by having fun, but by finding ways to take his inventions to market. Many people wrongly assume that Edison invented the light bulb. He didn't. He experimented with what others had already done and found a way to make his bulb last longer, but unlike other inventors, Edison also found a way to take it to market and sell it. I'm sure that gave him a lot of joy.

#TENWORDS

CHRISTIAN DIOR

"A person who only sees fashion in fashion is foolish".

Steve Jobs' design brief to the iMac designers of *"Make it like a sunflower"* was inspired by Christian Dior's creative brief to his perfumier's in 1947 which simply suggested, *"Make it smell like love"*.

Fashion designers don't use words to tell their stories, they use fabrics, fragrances, form and design. And then, summoning all the creative inspiration that they can find, they share their fabricated stories with the world by hosting theatrical runway shows which showcase the uniqueness of their brand. Often not a word is spoken, but the audiences understand that they are watching a story unfold. A story which is about so much more than the satisfaction of wearing an exclusive designer label.

Nobody in fashion ever understood this more than Christian Dior. I didn't realise how powerful some of Dior's stories were until one of them hit me like a train in early 2017. I was in Las Vegas to speak at a marketing conference and in between sessions, I wondered into Dior on *"The Strip"* eager to see their newest collection. In the corner of the store was a distraught man being given a glass of water. There was quite a commotion. It turned out that he had recently lost his business and his wife, and had little interest in living anymore. He had gone to Vegas *"to go out in style"* and take his own life. Eager to comfort the gentleman, Dior's store 'ambassadors' distracted the man by telling him stories about the celebrities that came into the store and the clothes that they bought. Celebrity stories turned into stories about why Christian Dior created the brand and what seemed like an eternity later (but was

READ: *Dior* by Dior
WATCH: *Dior & I* by Frédéric Tcheng
FOLLOW: @Dior

#**TEN**WORDS

CHRISTIAN DIOR

Probably little over an hour), the gentleman was trying on clothes from the store and looking carefully at himself in the mirror. The 'ambassador' a gorgeous man called Oscar, spoke to us about how your clothes are your suit of armour, and so much more than just material, buttons and zips.

Christian Dior once said that he wished to make people, "*not only more beautiful, but also happier*".

Desperate to see how this particular story played out I stayed in the store trying on clothes myself, and watching the gentleman respectfully from across the store. By the time he was ready to leave, his voice had changed and his melancholic tones had become much lighter. His shoulders which were previously down and slumped now looked strong and upright. And the battered suitcase which he dragged into the store was being taken away and placed in the trash, at his request, because he didn't want any reminders of his past life anymore. Taking just the essentials from his luggage, the gentleman left the store that day with an entirely new wardrobe and a renewed passion for life.

My words can not even begin to do this story justice because this simple window shopping trip saved this mans life. As I left the store, Oscar reminded me of our earlier conversation. "So *some people don't want relationships with brands anymore*". Looking at the gentleman who we could still make out in the distance, strutting confidently down the strip in his new armour, Oscar turned to me and said, *"That man will have a relationship with Dior for the rest of his life"*.

#TENWORDS

WALT DISNEY

"You reach a point where you don't work for money".

"If you can dream it you can do it... Whatever you do, do it well. Do it so well that when people see you do it they will want to come back and see you do it again and they will want to bring others and show them how well you do what you do".

Walt Disney

READ: *Walt Disney* by Neil Gabler
WATCH: *Saving Mr. Banks* with Emma Thompson
FOLLOW: @DisneyWords

Looking back over Walt Disney's life forces you to re-imagine what can be achieved in a lifetime. In just 65 years, Disney had revolutionised filmmaking, created an entertainment empire that won 22 Oscars from 59 nominations, and built what was to become the world's most successful theme park. Disney even held the patent for Technicolor for two years, making him the only animator allowed to make colour animated films! The most important film Disney would ever make was Snow White. Work started on the movie on August 9, 1934, and it would take 1,400 people over four years to finish it. Determined to create *"an emotional masterpiece"*, Disney gave his team twenty-one pages of notes and used collaborative storyboards for the very first time. He was convinced that mapping out the narrative of the film would help to understand exactly which parts of the story were most likely to receive the strongest emotional reactions from the audience. The process became so expensive as new scenes were added and lengthy sequences were deleted that many industry analysts predicted that the movie would bankrupt Disney. Despite it going way over budget and costing $1.5 million, Snow White went on to make over $418 million. Trusting his heart paid off. Not only did Snow White become one of the world's most commercially successful movies, but 80 years after it was first released, it is still regarded as the greatest animated movie of all time.

#TENWORDS

Snow White was the first feature film to involve a storyboard. People assumed it was used to reduce expensive animation costs, but Walt Disney used it in order to figure out which were the places in the movie where people would laugh, cry or be scared.

#**TEN**WORDS

CORY DOCTOROW

"Complaining about the universe's unfairness is not a successful strategy".

Cory Doctorow is a wonderfully smart science fiction writer of books such as *With a Little Help* and *For the Win, Makers*. I first discovered him through his copyright law manifesto, *"Information Doesn't Want To Be Free"* a book which he published for free under a creative commons licence at archive.org. It's a superb read which inspires like-minded souls to continue campaigning for digital rights. He writes beautifully about how creators should protect their work and how they should campaign for themselves. Here are his five writing tips to help *you* create better content for whatever *"cause"* it is that you feel most passionate about.

1. Write every day. Anything you do every day gets easier. If you're insanely busy, make the amount that you write every day small (10 words? 100 words?) but do it every day.
2. Write even when the mood isn't right. You can't tell if what you're writing is good or bad while you're writing it.
3. Write when the book sucks and it isn't going anywhere. Just keep writing. It doesn't suck. Your conscious is having a panic attack because it doesn't believe your subconscious knows what it's doing.
4. Stop in the middle of a sentence, leaving a rough edge for you to start from the next day — that way, you can write three or five words without being *"creative"* and before you know it, you're writing.
5. Write even when the world is chaotic. You don't need a cigarette, silence, music, a comfortable chair, or inner peace to write. You just need ten minutes and a writing implement.

Cory Doctorow is a Canadian-British blogger, journalist, and science fiction author. He is also an activist in favour of liberalising copyright laws and the Creative Commons organization, using some of their licenses for his books. He is a super smart guy who writes eloquently about digital rights management, file sharing, and post-scarcity economics.

READ: Information Doesn't Want To Be Free
SUBSCRIBE: BoingBoing.net
FOLLOW: @Doctorow | @EFF

#**TEN**WORDS

JULIA DONALDSON

"A mouse took a stroll through the deep dark wood…"

Inspiration can strike you anywhere, at any time. When Julia Donaldson was in her late twenties, she wrote songs for the BBC TV children's programs that I used to watch when I was growing up. She was always looking for her "*big break*" but it wasn't until Julia was 47 that inspiration struck her in the most remarkable way. Researching ideas for an educational series of plays based on traditional tales, Julia came across a version of a Chinese story about a little girl who escapes being eaten by a tiger by claiming to be the fearsome Queen of the Jungle and inviting him to walk behind her. The tiger misinterprets the terror of the various animals they meet as being related to her rather than him and flees.

Julia sensed that this story was too important to be just an educational aid so she decided to turn it into a picture book with illustrator Axel Scheffler. The girl became a mouse, jungle creatures were turned into woodland animals, and the tiger evolved into a monster reminiscent of a buffalo but "a lot scarier". And that's how *The Gruffalo* was born! By 2014 sales topped £10m in the UK, making her (according to Nielsen) the only author to ever record five years in a row of eight-figure revenue. Apart from *The Gruffalo* (13M copies sold) Julia has now written over 180 books and has become a Children's Laureate. Proof that anyone can stumble across inspiration but remarkable things can happen if you *act* on it.

Since I started speaking to large audiences at Adobe I have carried a small Gruffalo with me in my bag everywhere. It's a silly thing and maybe some kind of comfort blanket, but I place him on the lectern to calm my nerves when I am presenting. I like that he also reminds me (like his creators Julia and Axel), that anything is possible when you put your mind to it.

READ: *The Gruffalo* by Julia Donaldson
WATCH: Julia's London Book Fair Interview 2011
FOLLOW: @TheRealGruffalo

#**TEN**WORDS

JACK DORSEY

"Connect people instantly to what is most meaningful to them".

"My goal is to simplify complexity... and it's really complex to make something simple!"

Jack Dorsey, Co-Founder of Twitter and Square

READ: *Hatching Twitter* by Nick Bilton
WATCH: Jack's Keynote at Columbia University (2013)
FOLLOW: @Jack

When Twitter was founded by @Jack Dorsey, @Biz Stone, @Evan Williams and @Noah Glass, they argued over what its' purpose should be. Twitter seemed like a powerful media tool for real-time news updates, but it also looked like it could become a powerful social network? If so, should it be about you (like Facebook) or about those around you instead? *"What are you doing?"* v *"What's happening?"* It was a small detail but one that made a big difference when defining Twitter's true purpose. The team agreed that Twitter's point of difference was supposed to be connecting people instantly to meaningful things which were happening around them. A few years later Jack was giving an interview in a coffee shop opposite my office, where he gave some great advice and provided more context to his ten words:

1. Never act as if you've made it.
2. Constantly innovate. You need to learn something new every day, otherwise you will just end up with a small interesting company rather than one that will change the world.
3. Don't be precious about your ideas. Don't keep them in your head. Surround yourself with the right people and talk them through. If you are a coder, then program it, if you're a developer then get it built immediately...
4. Having first mover advantage is over-rated. MySpace was a first mover.
5. It's more important to have an idea BEST than have it FIRST. There is always room for disruption.
6. Constantly better yourself to stay ahead of the game.

#**TEN**WORDS

JACK DORSEY

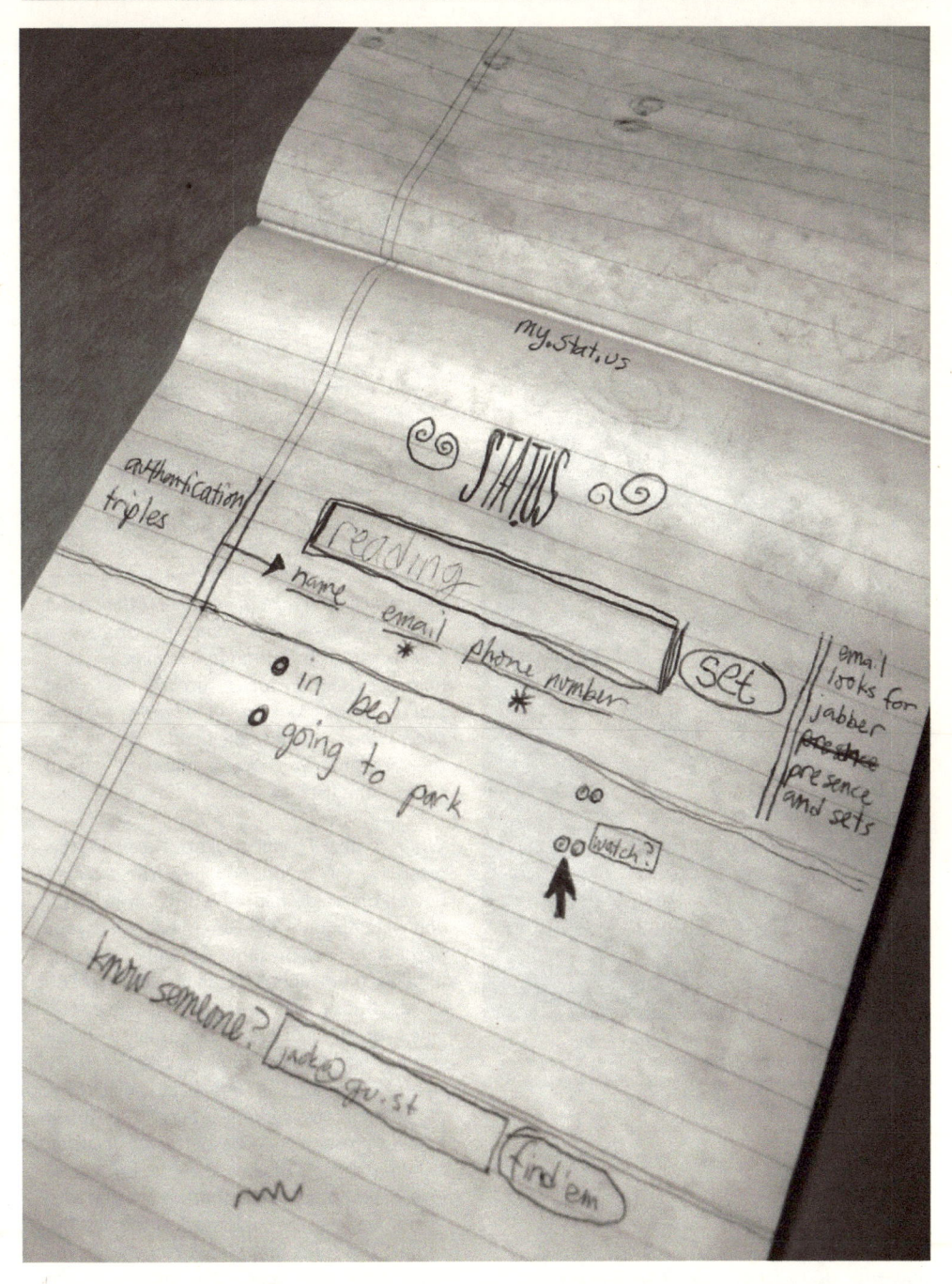

The first ever diagram of what Twitter might look like, taken from Jack Dorsey's notebook after a brainstorming session with co-founders Evan Williams, Biz Stone and Noah Glass.

#TENWORDS

NANCY DUARTE

"Think of slides as billboards with 3 second attention spans".

"When you read a piece of information, three days later you remember 10% of it. Add a strong picture and you'll remember 65%". Nancy Duarte quoting research from University of Washington biologist John Medina.

READ: *The Storytellers Secret* by Carmine Gallo
WATCH: *The Secret Structure of Great Talks* (TED)
FOLLOW: @NancyDuarte

If you want to create visually interesting slides, less is more. Presentation expert, author and superstar TED speaker Nancy Duarte recommends following a three-second rule. If viewers do not understand the gist of your slide in three seconds, it's too complicated. "*Think of your slides as billboards,*" says Duarte. "*When people drive, they only briefly take their eyes off their main focus, which is the road, to process a billboard of information. Similarly, your audience should focus intently on what you're saying, looking only briefly at your slides when you display them.*" When was the last time you saw a billboard with a bullet-point list?

When I heard Nancy Duarte explain this properly, she mentioned how the average PowerPoint slide had 40 words on it, but if you watch people like Elon Musk, Steve Jobs or Sundar Pichai present, you will notice that it takes them about 12 slides to reach 40 words. And if they are anything like Simon Sinek or Bryan Stevenson, they will tell stories and not have any slides at all. Nancy Duarte has lots of practical advice for presenters. She travels around the world helping presenters to be better by focusing on many aspects of what they do, but what I love most about her is that no matter who she is training, her message is always the same. "*This is not about you! You are not the hero who will save the audience;* **the audience is your hero**".

#TENWORDS

ROBIN DUNBAR

"Most humans are unable to sustain more than 150 friendships".

Robin Dunbar (*Anthropologist-in-Chief at Oxford University and creator of Dunbar's Number*) first got curious about the number 150 when he noticed that it was the optimum size for factory departments, Neolithic farming villages, the basic unit size of Roman armies and the size at which a local community needed some kind or organisational body to help it govern or police itself.

READ: How Many Friends Does One Person Need?
WATCH: *Can the internet buy you more friends?* TEDx
FOLLOW: 150 people.

The biggest social revolution of the last decade has not been a great political event, but the way our social world has been redefined by social networks such as MySpace, Facebook, Twitter, Whatsapp and Snapchat. In the past, the reach of our personal networks was dictated mostly by the people that we met in person on a regular basis. Today our friendship groups extend into the thousands. But how many friends does one person really need? And what's the maximum amount of friends that a human being can sustain? These are great questions that Robin Dunbar has answered scientifically, based upon extensive research he undertook by studying the social structures of Chimpanzees.

Extrapolating the size of the neocortex in our brains compared to that of a primate, Dunbar asserted that the optimum group size for human relationships is 150 – this being the number meaningful relationships a person can sustain at any one time. Dunbar claims that within those 150 relationships, as new people arrive, other people (often without realising it) leave. He argues that most of us only have around 5 close friends who know everything about us. Up to 10 friends who we would go on holiday with. And up to 50 who we enjoy spending time with, but usually no more than 100 people who know our daily lives. It makes you wonder, not just what is a *"friend"* but how many friends does one person *really* need?

It's better to have 100 people LOVE you than 1,000,000 people who kinda LIKE you.

BRIAN CHESKY

#TENWORDS

BOB DYLAN

"All I can do is be me, whoever that is".

Bob Dylan didn't show up to his own high school graduation party, so when he initially didn't acknowledge the fact that he had won the Nobel Prize for literature in 2017, the organising committee shouldn't have been so surprised. Regarded by many as the best storytelling singer-songwriter of all time, Bob Dylan epitomises everything that ten words is supposed to be about. The big idea, communicated via a few short sentences, containing short words that the average person enjoys and understands. Dylan has built an incredible career upon telling short stories, recording 38 studio albums and using his words as protest songs, campaigning for the Civil Rights Movement and anti-war movement via songs such as "*Blowin' in the Wind*" and "*The Times They Are a-Changin'*".

Dylan's albums such as Highway 61 Revisited, Blonde on Blonde and The Freewheelin' Bob Dylan have changed peoples lives. And his music, applied to his lyrics, have taken his words to a place that they wouldn't have gone on their own. Some stories need to be sung, not told. So when Dylan received news of his Nobel prize and had the chance to ponder what it meant, he eventually replied, "*Songs are unlike literature. They're meant to be sung, not read. I hope some of you get the chance to listen to these lyrics the way they were intended to be heard: in concert or on record or however people are listening to songs these days*".

"What's money? A man is a success if he gets up in the morning and goes to bed at night and in between does what he wants to do". Bob Dylan

READ: Bob Dylan's Nobel Prize Lecture
LISTEN: *This is: Bob Dylan* (Spotify Playlist)
FOLLOW: Your own path.

#TENWORDS

THOMAS EDISON

"I haven't failed. I've found 10,000 ways that don't work".

Thomas Edison lived an impressive life. He is most famous for inventing* the light bulb, but that is just one small part of his legacy. Edison also invented the phonograph, making it possible to record spoken voice for the first time and play it back. He created one of the first motion picture players, a vote recorder, an iron ore separator, the telegraph, an electric pen, the carbon telephone, fuel cell technology and the alkaline battery. He even represented artists who appeared on his phonographs, making him one of the world's first talent agents. Much has been written of Thomas Edison's life and what he accomplished during it, but less has been written about how he did it. Edison *loathed* sleep! Consider this note he wrote in his journal in 1921 after studying various British Medical Journals,

"Most people overeat 100 per cent, and oversleep 100 per cent, because they like it. That extra 100 per cent makes them unhealthy and inefficient. The person who sleeps eight or ten hours a night is never fully asleep and never fully awake. For myself I never found need of more than four or five hours' sleep. I never dream. It's real sleep. We are always hearing people talk about 'loss of sleep' as a calamity. They better call it loss of time, vitality and opportunities".

So the next time you think you don't have enough hours in the day to get things done or *"make a difference"*, why not try taking Edison's advice and set your alarm clock a few hours earlier!

When Thomas Edison opened his research laboratory in Menlo Park in 1876, he declared at a press conference that his "Ideas Lab" would generate, "One minor invention every 10 days and a big thing every 6 months!". He did more than that., he invented many things we still use today. (IBM has over 380,000 employees and registered over 8,088 patents in 2016. Edison registered 1,093 patents on his own!)

READ: *Wizard of Menlo Park* by Walter Isaacson
WATCH: The Thomas Edison Documentary
FOLLOW: His work ethic.

* Edison innovated on a previous version of the light bulb but was credited with inventing it when he found a commercially viable way to take it to market.

#TENWORDS

ALBERT EINSTEIN

"Only a life lived for others is a life worthwhile".

When asked to speak about *"relativity"* for a Yale University review Einstein replied, *"When a man sits with a pretty girl for an hour, it seems like a minute. But let him sit on a hot stove for a minute — and it's longer than any hour. That's relativity."*

READ: *The World As I See It* by Albert Einstein
WATCH: *Einstein* on National Geographic
FOLLOW: @AlbertEinstein

Albert Einstein needs no introduction. He was one of the world's greatest thinkers and the first celebrity scientist, partially due to the fact that he was so quotable. Much has been written about his work, his famous equations and his views around quantum physics, but less has been mentioned about the way that he communicated his ideas. Einstein loved short sentences. He loved the elegance of a short equation. And he loved being able to make his work relevant to the average person. In one interview, he dropped his famous quote, *"If you can't explain it simply, you don't understand it well enough"*. He loved that quote and repeated it many times but my favourite version is, *"If you can't explain your physics to a barmaid in a language that she understands, then you don't understand it well enough"*.

"Make things simpler but not simple", Einstein used to tell his students, and if there is one theme running through this book, it would be that. In my mind, Einstein is the patron saint of big ideas, small words and short sentences. He is one of the few people who inspires people across every industry and profession to work hard, love longer and explain their work more simply. Because what I love most about Einstein is the ten words I chose for him. When you have discovered $E=mc^2$ you can do pretty much anything you want, but to his credit, Einstein never lost sight of the fact that he was living his life to educate and inspire others.

Make it simple.

But significant.

DON DRAPER

#TENWORDS

JIMMY FALLON

"Find common ground with the person you are speaking to".

"'Have fun' is my message. Be silly. You're allowed to be silly. There's nothing wrong with it". Jimmy Fallon

READ: *Saturday Night Live: The Book*
WATCH: *The Tonight Show* with Jimmy Fallon
FOLLOW: @JimmyFallon

When Clint Eastwood appeared on The Tonight Show to promote the musical *Jersey Boys*, Fallon said, *"I love the music. I love the characters. My parents are from Brooklyn and we knew people like this. The way it was shot, the cars, the scenery, it reminded me of my parents' wedding photo."* Fallon reached behind his desk and pulled out an old photo of his parents walking hand-in-hand in a neighbourhood that looked liked it was set in the movie. Fallon may have little in common with Eastwood, but in that moment they shared a mutual love for the period in which the movie was based. Celebrities and interesting people from all walks of life enjoy Fallon because he enjoys talking to them. Jimmy Fallon is fun to watch because he's so genuinely interested in his guests. And that makes Fallon likeable, which is why he's dominating the late night ratings.

Once Fallon finds common ground, he lets his guests shine. When someone says something even remotely funny, Fallon laughs the loudest. Jimmy was once asked for the secret to his success. *"What made you such a successful TV host?"* the interviewer asked. Jimmy replied with, you guessed it, ten words, *"Find common ground with the person you are speaking to"*. He then explained how he asked questions but spent 75% of the conversation listening to their answers, hoping to make them feel as though they were the funniest and most important person in the room. *[Applause].*

#TENWORDS

JON FAVREAU

"The best way to connect with people is through stories".

Obama is without question one of the world's finest speakers, but much of the credit needs to go to his speech-writer of eight years, Jon Favreau. I have heard Jon give many interviews over the years and have kept notes from his advice, so here's his top five tips to help tell better stories:

1. The Story Is More Important Than The Words.
"In my experience communications to often focuses on finding the right words. Of course, words are important but the first question you have to ask yourself is: 'What is the story I'm trying to sell?'"

2. Keep It Simple.
"Long speeches are the easiest to write. They are also the most forgettable. Audiences today can only handle so much information before they start losing focus. You should aim at twenty minutes max. That requires tremendous discipline, especially if you're in an organisation with a lot of people in the mix. But remember that a speech about everything is a speech about nothing. Narrow your story down to the essential point."

3. Always Address The Arguments Against Your Position During Your Presentation, Not After.
Think about the **objections** you will encounter and don't wait until the Q&A to answer them.

4. Empathy is Key.
"You have to know what the world looks like when you are in their shoes." Successful speeches are easy to understand and address the issues that the audience is facing.

5. There Is No Persuasion Without Inspiration
Emotion is the most important element of motivating an audience. "*The best way to connect with people is through stories that are important to people's lives*".

"Waste no words. You have only about 200 words to say something memorable. Don't waste any on how you never thought you'd win, or didn't prepare a speech. Instead of reciting a checklist of names, spend a few words on one person who helped make it possible for you to stand on that stage. Thank the rest later with a heartfelt note — or money". Jon's advice to Oscar winners on writing acceptance speeches.

READ: Obama's New Hampshire "*Yes We Can*" Speech
WATCH: *The Language of Presidential Speech Writing*
FOLLOW: @JonFavs

#TENWORDS

TIM FERRISS

"If you're wasting time having fun, you're not wasting time".

My Top 5 Tim Ferris podcast episodes:
1. Tony Robbins
2. Seth Godin
3. Scott Adams
4. Jocko Willink
5. Kevin Costner (yes, really)

READ: *Tools of Titans* by Tim Ferriss
LISTEN: *The Tim Ferris podcast*
WATCH: Tim's *"Stoic"* TED Talk (2017)
FOLLOW: @TFerriss

Tim has introduced me to many of the people in this book through his podcast and his books. He is one of the most selfless, obsessive and brilliant people I have ever met. He also has a dark past and openly talks about the depression which almost caused him to take his own life. Fast Company calls him one of the world's most innovative people and Forbes magazine say that he is one of *the* names you *need* to know. He was an early stage investor in Uber, Facebook and Alibaba and is the author of three number one New York Times and Wall Street Journal best sellers. Not too shabby for a guy who just started out wanting to tell other people's stories.

Tim is most famous (and most commercially successful) for his *"4-Hour"* books but it is his podcasts which inspire me the most. I can't recommend them highly enough. They have been downloaded over 100 million times, not just because he is a fascinating character, but because he does such a superb job of curating conversations with people who will genuinely change your life. Tim is the master of the short story, and well versed in captivating hearts and minds with his punchy powerful advice, but what impresses me the most is that he has built such a level of trust with his audience. In a world of short attention spans, the *"engagement rates"* for Tim's podcasts (often over 2 hours long) are among the highest on iTunes. Listen to him. Learn from him. Thank me later.

#TENWORDS

HENRY FORD

"Quality means doing it right when no one is looking".

In 2012 Fortune magazine voted Henry Ford's decision to double the wages of his workers as the greatest business decision of all time. Despite being widely criticised as commercial suicide at the time, Ford believed that *"one's own employees ought to be one's own best customers"*. His decision to increase wages from $2.50 to $5 per day in 1914 not only allowed employees to afford their own car, but it also boosted morale, increased loyalty and became the catalyst which turned Ford into a global success.

READ: Fortune: Great Business Decisions
WATCH: Henry Ford: Model T Documentary
FOLLOW: @Ford

Henry Ford became obsessed with cars on June 4th 1896 when he drove a horseless carriage for the first time. Over the next three years, he built a team of thirteen engineers and founded The Detroit Automobile Company. Fifty-seven car companies were founded the same year as Ford's, with another one hundred launching the following year, but none had a vision as big as Henry's. Securing investment from wealthy businessmen, Ford set about building a car that would be commercially viable but divisions soon grew between Ford's investors and his master plan. Ford wanted to build a car for *everyone*. The investors wanted to make a car aimed at the upper classes. The investors not only had a different vision to Ford, but their impatience meant that they didn't have the same obsession with tiny details either. Henry needed to solve design problems which would make his car superior to his competitors, but he was under pressure from investors to build a car quickly and get it to market first. In a devious stroke of genius, Ford got his workers to build parts for cars that he never planned to use, in order to buy time from investors. He wanted to build *"a car for the people"*, not just a car for wealthy people. Investors soon realised what was going on and backed out, but it left Henry free to build the Ford Motor Company. Ford promised himself that never again would he take orders from anyone who asked him to compromise on quality.

#TENWORDS

HENRY FORD

Ford Model T Light Delivery Car

Demand for Ford Cars Doubles Annually

100,000 Ford Cars Are in Service Now

$700

Fully Equipped with
Automatic Brass Windshield
Speedometer
Three Oil Lamps
Two Gas Lamps
Generator
Horn
Tools

FORD Model T Light Delivery Car

Business everywhere demands such a car as this Ford Model T Light Delivery Car. Business demanded it because it needed a simple, economical and reliable means of handling light loads. It has been proved that the Model T will fill the want because of its five years of splendid service in the pleasure car class, where it demonstrated its strength and general utility in every test.

The Delivery Car is built on the same Ford Model T Chassis that has established such world-wide fame for all-around efficiency and economy. That chassis, which because of its excellence of design and its light weight, does from 20 to 25 miles on one gallon of gasoline.

Business men will recognize in the Model T's simplicity of operation, and in its freedom from tire troubles a particular adaptability to commercial purposes.

Mounted on the Model T chassis is a handsome, roomy body of steel. It carries 750 pounds of Merchandise with ease and at any speed desired.

The John Wanamaker stores in New York and Philadelphia use fifty of these Ford Model T delivery cars. In the service of those great merchandising establishments, the Model T delivery cars have proved of the utmost efficiency and economy. The Bell Telephone Company uses over 100 Ford Model T cars in its service throughout America. Investigation and long tests proved that no other car would do such satisfactory work so cheaply as the Ford Model T.

No method of light deliveries has ever been tested which proved so satisfactorily to the Ford Model T Light Delivery Car system.

Immediate delivery assured.

Branches in All Principal Cities — *Ford Motor Company* — DETROIT, MICHIGAN, U.S.A.

The Ten-Millionth Ford

The 10,000,000th Ford car left the Highland Park factories of the Ford Motor Company June 4. This is a production achievement unapproached in automotive history. Tremendous volume has been the outgrowth of dependable, convenient, economical service.

Ford Motor Company
Detroit, Michigan

Runabout $265   Coupe $525   Tudor Sedan $590   Fordor Sedan $685
All prices f. o. b. Detroit

SEE THE NEAREST AUTHORIZED FORD DEALER

The Touring Car
$295
F. O. B. Detroit
Demountable Rims and Starter $85 extra

Ford Newspaper 73
800 lines—Week of June 8, 1924

#TENWORDS

TOM FORD

"If it's not fun, I don't want to do it".

"Time and silence are the most luxurious things today".

"I love communicating with people through what I create. But also enhancing their lives. Giving them something that should bring joy. And fun". Tom Ford

READ: *Tom Ford* by Tom Ford
WATCH: *Visionaries: Tom Ford* (OWN)
FOLLOW: @TomFord

Tom Ford is the hardest working man in fashion. He hustled from the very beginning. His career kicked off after applying for work at some of Paris' most famous fashion houses telling them he had graduated from the famous fashion college Parsons School of Design in Paris. He wasn't lying. He did graduate from Parsons, he just neglected to tell everyone that he graduated in architecture, not fashion. Within a decade, Tom was the hottest (and hardest working) designer in fashion, running both Gucci and Yves Saint Laurent at the same time. *"If I'm awake, I'm working... but you have to love what you do to the point that you can't imagine doing anything else with your life"*.

This is why Tom's ten word philosophy is so powerful, because if you're going to work 18 hours a day and commit to producing 16 collections each year, you *need* to enjoy what you're doing or you're not going to last very long. Or be very good. Some people want to change their industry. Others want to leave a legacy. Tom Ford is different.

"From the time we're born until we die, we're kept busy with artificial stuff that isn't important... we promote materialism which is ultimately not the thing that brings you happiness. Nothing lasts. And that's in a way the beauty of it all. Once you can accept that. You'll be ok. So I'm not going to do anything that is not fun".

TOM FORD

I had the pleasure of speaking at an event with Tom Ford and the British Fashion Council in June 2017. It was a wonderful event with a roomful of senior executives hanging on his every word as he reminisced about his life, regretting nothing, and being thankful for everything. I was happy just to be there, listening to one of the people I admire the most sharing his views about life, love, fashion and technology, but then something amazing happened. Something especially amazing considering that this book was in the final stages of being written and I was working on a challenging situation at work. Tom shared with the small group assembled in that room the one piece of advice that was the secret to his success. And yes, of course it was ten words long.

"You just have to find a way to make it sexy".

Tom was talking about a difficult stage, early in his career when he took over at Gucci, a luxury fashion house which at the time was in the middle of great turmoil. The business was going through a transformation, the boardroom was rife with politics and different agendas, many in the industry saw Gucci as an irrelevant brand that only old ladies still wore, and many within the company had been there many years and had no intention of changing their mindset. But then in walked Tom Ford, with the freedom to re-invent the brand, and no senior executives taking sufficient notice of his part of the business to care what he did. Armed with these ten words, Tom did exactly what Tom does best. He made Gucci sexy. He ran provocative campaigns. He introduced sexual themes that challenged the way fashion campaigns were supposed to run. He put Kate Moss on the runway and he asked a curvy Sophie Dahl to pose naked with a bottle of perfume. Within the decade that he was there, Gucci grew to $4 billion in sales, bought Yves St. Laurent, grew even further to hit $10 billion, and the rest, as they say, is a Harvard Business School case study.

So when Tom told me that I needed to make IBM sexy, I thought he was joking. He wasn't. Any brand, whether luxury fashion or luxury technology, survives by telling emotional stories, having a strong point of view and showing people what you believe they should be doing next year or next season. It was sublime advice that I will never forget. So whatever *you* do, whether it is selling software or expensive clothes, you just *have* to find a way to make it sexy...

#TENWORDS

BENJAMIN FRANKLIN

"Either write something worth reading or do something worth writing".

Founding Father of the United States. Renowned polymath and a leading author, printer, political theorist, politician, freemason, postmaster, scientist, inventor, civic activist, statesman, and diplomat. Not a bad CV. No wonder Ben Franklin needed schemes and routines to get everything done.

READ: *Benjamin Franklin* by Walter Isaacson
WATCH: *Benjamin Franklin* PBS TV mini-series
FOLLOW: Your own routine

In his autobiography, Benjamin Franklin famously outlined a scheme to achieve *"moral perfection"* according to a thirteen-week plan. Each week was devoted to a particular virtue:

1. Temperance
2. Silence
3. Order
4. Resolution
5. Frugality
6. Industry
7. Sincerity
8. Justice
9. Moderation
10. Cleanliness
11. Tranquility
12. Chastity
13. Humility

His offences against these virtues were tracked on his calendar, which he designed in 1726 when he was 20. He wanted to lead a *"significant life"*, so he designed a routine and a scheme that could help him achieve it. Franklin thought if he could maintain his devotion to one virtue for an entire week, it would become a habit; then he could move onto the next virtue, successively making fewer and fewer black offences (*indicated on the calendar by a black mark*) until he had completely reformed himself and would thereafter need only occasional bouts of moral maintenance. When asked why a routine was so important to him, Franklin replied with another ten words, *"Never leave that till tomorrow which you can do today"*.

#**TEN**WORDS

BENJAMIN FRANKLIN

Ten Words!

The morning question, What good shall I do this day?	5	Rise, wash, and address *Powerful Goodness*; contrive day's business and take the resolution of the day; prosecute the present study; and breakfast.
	6	
	7	
	8	
	9	Work.
	10	
	11	
	12	Read or overlook my accounts, and dine.
	1	
	2	
	3	Work.
	4	
	5	
	6	Put things in their places, supper, music, or diversion, or conversation; examination of the day.
	7	
	8	
	9	
Evening question, What good have I done today?	10	
	11	
	12	
	1	Sleep.
	2	
	3	
	4	

In his autobiography written in 1791, Benjamin Franklin shared his daily routine (beginning with a ten word question) in order to try and encourage his readers to live more meaningful and productive lives.

#TEN WORDS

BILL GATES

"Your most unhappy customers are your greatest source of learning".

"Intellectual property has the shelf life of a banana... In three years, every product my company makes will be obsolete. The only question is whether we will make them obsolete or somebody else will... 'If it ain't broke don't fix it' doesn't apply anymore because if it ain't broke it's obsolete".

READ: *The Innovators* by Walter Isaacson
WATCH: *Pirates of Silicon Valley*
FOLLOW: @BillGates

Bill Gates is an innovator. According to some definitions, that means he took something that already existed and found a way to take it to market, faster than anybody else, and in a better or more commercial format. Bill has a different definition of an innovator though, "*An innovator is probably a fanatic, somebody who loves what they do, works day and night, may ignore normal things to some degree and therefore be viewed as a bit imbalanced*". Gates was also a rebel with little respect for authority or the status quo, another trait of innovators.

This never manifested itself more so than when Bill took his Windows operating system to market, challenging companies like IBM with the philosophy that the money was in the software, not hardware. Unlike his "friend" and fierce rival Steve Jobs, Gates chose to release his software when it wasn't perfect. He didn't mind so much about the elegance of the icons. Jobs believed that people didn't not know what they wanted until you showed them and when you did, it needed to work perfectly. Gates preferred to get to market first, albeit with an inferior product, with the hope of making it perfect through patches and updates based on the feedback of unhappy users discovering bugs. Bill won the software battle, not because he was smarter or his product was better, but because he was more interested in listening to his most unhappy customers, instead of telling them what they wanted.

#**TEN**WORDS

STEFANI "LADY GAGA" GERMANOTTA

"We need fantasy to survive because reality is too difficult".

"You have to be unique and different, and shine in your own way". Stefani *"Lady Gaga"* Germanotta

Stefani started her career dancing in burlesque clubs at the age of 16. She wanted to be a singer but was rejected by record labels for *"being too theatrical"*. Turning to the stage, she was rejected by Broadway for being *"too pop"*. Refusing to compromise she *"invented"* Lady Gaga. The rest is history.

LISTEN: *The Fame* by Lady Gaga
WATCH: Lady Gaga's set at Glastonbury (2009)
FOLLOW: @LadyGaga

When Stefani Germanotta, aka *"Lady Gaga"* was booked to play Glastonbury festival in 2009, everyone knew she would be good, they just didn't know how good. Within a year she had sold over 8 million albums and 35 million singles, had been nominated for six Grammy's and three Brit Awards – as well as becoming the first artist to have four number one singles from her debut album *The Fame*.

But it's not just Gaga's theatrical storytelling and bouncy songs that got her to where she is today, it was her dedication to building a *"personal brand"*. I hate that phrase because it reminds me of all things *Kardashian* and superficial, but Gaga was one of the first artists to leverage social media by building *"her brand"* around a community of fans who she refers affectionately to as *"little monsters"*. She built that community on trust as one of the first artists who allowed fans to post content about her without any threat of copyright infringement. She also spent more time chatting to her fans than she did posting about herself. And to make sure that her shows had enough *"fantasy"* to inspire her *monsters*, she created her own production studio *"The Haus of Gaga"* modelled upon Andy Warhol's *Factory*. This allows her to build whatever stage sets she wants, even if she has an idea at the last minute. She really is one of a kind. Beautiful, brilliantly talented, and a bit mad. The music industry is a better place because she is in it.

#TENWORDS

SETH GODIN

"The leader is the leader because they did something remarkable".

Ever since 2002, Seth has written a blog post every day, driven by the hope that his thoughts and ideas might inspire marketers to make a difference in their work. He is in my opinion, the most influential (and relevant) marketer on the planet, yet he ironically doesn't engage with his fans very much. He turned the comments off on his blog, he is not on Twitter and he doesn't speak in public very often. In a socially connected world where everybody is just one click away from everybody else, Seth takes a lot of criticism for being so detached from the marketing community. This may seem unusual for someone leading such a social industry, but few people realise that Seth is the world's greatest marketer *because* he refuses to be distracted by social networks and bland (brand) conversations. If you're going to support an audience of millions of marketers, all with very short attention spans, then you better make sure that you remove as many distractions as possible from your own life in order to give them something of quality and value every day.

Seth Godin is the world's greatest living marketer. He is the author of 17 books including Purple Cow (the book that this quote came from), which had more than 23 print runs in its first two years selling over 150,000 copies, something unheard of for a marketing book.

Seth generally writes no more than a few hundred words each day, but his words are powerful because he spends a lot of time thinking about them and communicates based on a simple motto: *"If you can't explain your position in less than eight words, then you don't have a position"*. Seth would think ten words are two too many.

READ: Purple Cow.
WATCH: Any of his interviews on YouTube.
FOLLOW: Seth's blog every day on Typepad.

#**TEN**WORDS

THE RULES OF MARKETING

WHO, PRECISELY, ARE YOU TRYING TO REACH?

WHAT CHANGE ARE YOU TRYING TO MAKE?

HOW WILL YOU KNOW IF IT'S WORKING?

HOW LONG BEFORE YOU WILL LOSE PATIENCE?

HOW LONG BEFORE SOMEONE ON YOUR TEAM GETS TO CHANGE THE MISSION?

HOW MUCH TIME AND MONEY ARE YOU PREPARED TO SPEND?

WHO GETS TO APPROVE THIS WORK?

WHO ARE YOU TRYING TO PLEASE OR IMPRESS?

SETH GODIN

#TENWORDS

BILLY GRAHAM

"Do not compromise your convictions for the sake of popularity".

"When I stand before an audience, I don't care whether it is in England or Ecuador, there are certain things I assume are in the audience already: Life's needs are not totally met by social improvement and material affluence - There is an essential emptiness in every life without Christ and only God can fill it - there is a universal fear of death". Every one of Billy messages spoke purely to those concerns.

READ: The Bible.
WATCH: Billy Graham: God's Ambassador
FOLLOW: (If you asked Billy): Jesus.

Billy Graham is one of the world's most famous evangelists. He was an evangelist in every sense of the world. Committing his life to preaching the gospel, Reverend Billy Graham spoke to over 215 million people in over 185 countries during his ministry. I was one of them. I'll never forget being on the pitch at Anfield football ground in Liverpool listening to him speak in 1984. I was 12 and I'd never before heard a speaker in front of such a huge audience speak as if he were just chatting to a few people in his lounge. His appeal was that he could connect with people unlike many other speakers before him or since. During 1973, an estimated 3.2 million people attended a Billy Graham Crusade in Seoul, South Korea, with 1.1 million travelling, mostly by foot to the final service on an airstrip. He impacted so many people simply because his preaching was directed to the average person. His vocabulary was always non-technical. His sentences were always short and simple.

"I've read the last page of the Bible. It's all going to turn out all right".

Billy Graham was unique but he didn't like talking about his celebrity status, preferring instead to shine a light on his beliefs. His legacy in popular culture is etched into stone though. Literally. As one of the 10 most admired men in the world (Gallup), Billy Graham became the 1000th person to have a star on the Hollywood Walk of Fame.

#**TEN**WORDS

BILLY GRAHAM

For over seventy years, Billy Graham stood close and spoke loud to over 215 million people in 185 countries.

#**TEN**WORDS

TIM GROVER

"You don't celebrate your achievements because you **always** want more".

Tim Grover has been Michael Jordan's personal trainer since the beginning of his career. He is the benchmark by which all other elite personal trainers are measured by. He tells all his athletes, *"Don't tell me the glass is half-full or half-empty; you either have something in that glass or you don't"*.

READ: *Relentless* by Tim Grover
WATCH: Grover training Jordan on YouTube
FOLLOW: @AttackAthletics

Most business leaders are not competitive enough. They need someone to push them harder, someone like Tim Grover. He's a badass performance coach who has changed the way that coaches support elite athletes. But then if you've been Michael Jordan's personal trainer for over twenty years, you probably know something about getting the best out of people. That extra 0.5% that turns a great athlete into the greatest of all-time. His techniques rely more upon mental strength than physical strength.

"Success isn't the same as talent...", I once heard him tell a group of executives attending one of his leadership courses, *"the world is full of incredibly talented people who never succeed at anything"*. Early on in Michael Jordan's career, he was already a superstar leading the league in scoring and appearing on the front cover of every sports magazine, but he wanted more. Inspired by Ali, Jordan wanted to be remembered as one of the greatest to ever play the game. Tim Grover helped Jordan develop the mental toughness needed to overcome all the challenges, personally and professionally, which helped him to become exactly that. Grover's training philosophy was always driven by these ten words. So when he was faced with Jordan questioning how he could become the greatest of all-time, Grover simply replied with another ten words, *"Everything you need to be great is already inside you"*.

#**TEN**WORDS

TIM GROVER

"Don't tell me about a workout that's 'easy' and done in 'the comfort of your own home'. Any workouts involving comfort aren't workouts. They're insults. You can work out at home, but if whatever you are doing makes you feel 'comfortable,' something is very wrong".

Tim Grover

#**TEN**WORDS

TOM HANKS

"Life is a grand adventure, so keep writing and reading".

Between 1994 and 2004, Tom Hanks was nominated for the most Academy Awards out of any actor. He was nominated for four and won two (*Forrest Gump* and *Philadelphia*). Tom lives in LA and writes about his grand life on the vintage typewriters that he collects.

READ: *I Am TOM* by Tom Hanks (New York Times)
WATCH: *Charlie Wilson's War* by Aaron Sorkin
DOWNLOAD: Hanx Writer

In 2006 Forbes made a list of the top 1,500 most trusted celebrities. Tom Hanks topped the list! He's come a long way from being broke and working as an intern for theatrical festivals. Hanks has now been acting for more than 30 years in more than 40 films and has won two Academy Awards. He often speaks about how the business is changing, paychecks aren't as big as they once were, studios are making fewer films and are pushing for more original content. But while the movie business has never been easy, I heard Hanks admit in an interview once, *"It's a lot more fun than many people on the inside let on. The secret that we all keep tucked in our pockets is that it's a great place to go every day. It's just more fun than fun can be. But we don't tell people that. We just talk about how hard the work is."*

We should all talk about how fun our jobs are (or could be) and less about how hard they are. So how did Hanks stay so positive early on in his career when he was fighting for his big break? The answer was one word. With two letters. *"No"*. Despite wanting to say yes to everything, Tom realized that, *"I had to start saying a very, very difficult word to people, which was 'no.' The odd lesson for that is, I figured out that's how you end up making favorable work. Saying yes, then you just work. But saying no means you made the choice of the type of story you wanted to tell and the type of character you want to play"*. Solid advice for all of us.

#**TEN**WORDS

TOM HANKS

"The sound of typing is one reason to own a vintage manual typewriter — alas, there are only three reasons, and none of them are ease or speed. In addition to sound, there is the sheer physical pleasure of typing; it feels just as good as it sounds, the muscles in your hands control the volume and cadence of the aural assault so that the room echoes with the staccato beat of your synapses. You can choose the typewriter to match your sound signature.

Remingtons from the 1930s go THICK THICK. Midcentury Royals sound like a voice repeating the word CHALK. CHALK. CHALK CHALK. Even the typewriters made for the dawning jet age (small enough to fit on the fold-down trays of the first 707s), like the Smith Corona Skyriter and the design masterpieces by Olivetti, go FITT FITT FITT like bullets from James Bond's silenced Walther PPK. Composing on a Groma, exported to the West from a Communist country that no longer exists, is the sound of work, hard work. Close your eyes as you touch-type and you are a blacksmith shaping sentences hot out of the forge of your mind".

I Am TOM by Tom Hanks (New York Times)

Tom Hanks believes that his words have more meaning when they are written on a manual typewriter. He writes scripts and thank you letters on one of the hundreds of vintage typewriters that he owns, sending out at least one hand typed note by snail mail every day.

#**TEN**WORDS

TINKER HATFIELD

"Athlete's with the right personality can challenge an entire sport".

Tinker Hatfield's art professor once told him that if people don't either love or hate your work, you haven't done anything. Ever since then, he tried to push the boundaries of shoe design, starting with the (clear air bubble) Air Max in 1987. Nike co-founder Phil Knight credits Tinker with almost single handedly saving Nike from bankruptcy in 1988 when he took over as head designer of the Air Jordan brand.

READ: *Shoe Dog* by Phil Knight
WATCH: *The Art of Design* S1:E2 (Netflix)
FOLLOW: @Nike

In 1984 I had a poster of Sebastian Coe on my wall and competed in the English Schools cross country championships wearing a pair of Nike Vainqueur's. In 1992 I bought a pair of Air Jordan VII's with my first paycheck, having been a Bull's fan since Jordan was drafted in 1984. In 1997 I took up golf after being captivated by Tiger's performance at the Masters and bought my first pair of golf shoes from NikeTown in Chicago. I ran my first 60 minute 10 mile in a pair of Nike Air Shox. The one thing that connects all these events and lies at the heart of my "relationship" with Nike? Each of those shoes were designed by Tinker Hatfield, Nike's head of design. And as a marketer, Tinker continues to inspire me today. His ten word quote *"The art of marketing is to get better every year"* is on the first page of all my notebooks. He believes that an athlete with the right personality can challenge the perception of the entire sport. Look at McEnroe. Agassi. Jordan. Ronaldo. Cantona. Armstrong. Schumacher. Woods. All of them challenged their sports. (For better *and* worse). All of them had shoes that reflected their personalities. And all of them were designed by Tinker Hatfield. Not bad for an architect who had never designed a shoe before working at Nike.

"I don't know if I have a legacy, but I will say that I'm proud of the fact that I'm from a small town in a small state and I've had more than a small impact". Tinker Hatfield

NIKE'S
11 MANAGEMENT MAXIMS

1. "*It is our nature to innovate.*" The company sees innovation as one of its core organizational competencies.
2. "*Nike is a company.*"
3. "*Nike is a brand.*" The "swoosh" logo is instantly recognizable around the world. Nike sees this as the symbol of its global leadership. It will enter only those markets that it thinks it can dominate. It says: 'If we can't lead it, we don't need it."
4. "*Simplify and go.*" Nike products have short life-cycles in terms both of technology and fashion. The company believes that making quick yet skillful decisions is key to its success. This aspect of Nike's vision, together with the seventh maxim, is particularly powerful in articulating the company's hugely successful use of emergent strategy.
5. "*The consumer decides.*" The company is keenly aware of the sophistication of its customers and it treats them as its key stakeholder.
6. "*Be a sponge.*" Employees at Nike are encouraged to be curious and open to new ideas, whatever their source.
7. "*Evolve immediately.*" Nike sees itself as being in perpetual motion—viewing change as a key source of innovation. This attitude can easily be observed in the wide range of products that Nike offers its consumers. It is another example of the company's use of emergent strategy to good effect.
8. "*Do the right thing.*" (Even when it's the hard thing). Nike thinks of itself as a responsible global citizen, embracing the stakeholder view of corporate social responsibility. It encourages its people to be honest and transparent and to promote diversity and sustainability.
9. "*Master the fundamentals.*" All the innovation in the world is useless if you can't put it into action. A crucial part of Nike's success is its ability to refine its performance—the recent growth in profits suggests that it's achieving this.
10. "*We are on the offense—always.*" To stay ahead in an extremely competitive environment, Nike urges its people to act like leaders in their field to achieve victory.
11. "*Remember the Man.*" The late Bill Bowerman is still held in high esteem throughout Nike, both for his understanding of athletes' needs and for his innovative spirit.

#TENWORDS

AUDREY HEPBURN

""Nothing is impossible because the word itself says, 'I'm possible'".

Hepburn spent 38 years of her life working with UNICEF. Before she died in 1993, she was awarded the Presidential Medal of Freedom for her work as a UN Goodwill Ambassador. The Audrey Hepburn Children's Fund has raised almost US$100 million to date. *"Makeup can only make you look pretty on the outside, but it doesn't help if you are ugly on the inside. Unless you eat the makeup."* Audrey Hepburn

READ: *Breakfast at Tiffany's* by Truman Capote
WATCH: *Roman Holiday* by William Wyler
FOLLOW: @UNICEF

Audrey Hepburn merchandise is everywhere. She's on bags, notebooks, mugs and you can't go a few clicks across Pinterest without seeing her face on something else. Such is the attraction of one of cinema's most iconic stars. But she never saw herself as an icon and never for one moment imagined it possible to become a movie star when she was growing up in war-torn Holland. During a pinup era graced by Marilyn Monroe and Rita Hayworth, Audrey Hepburn presented a very different kind of look. She once said about herself, *"I don't have sex appeal and I know it. As a matter of fact, I think I'm rather funny-looking. My teeth are funny for one thing, and I have none of the attributes usually required for a movie queen, including the shapeliness."* It didn't help that Audrey's mother used to frequently tell her that she was unattractive. But instead of changing her look, she embraced it.

I love Audrey not just because of her confidence and acting ability, but because she believed that laughter was the key to her success. *"Laugh as much as you can. I love people who make me laugh. I honestly think it's the thing I like most, to laugh. It cures a multitude of ills. It's probably the most important thing in a person."* Towards the end of her life, a journalist asked Audrey to sum up her incredible life and in her inimitable style, she simply replied with a beautifully short but pretty sentence, *"I think I've been particularly lucky."*

#**TEN**WORDS

REID HOFFMAN

"The value of your network should be your greatest asset".

"The person passionate about what he or she is doing will outwork and outlast the guy motivated solely by making money." Reid Hoffman

READ: *The Startup of You* by Reid Hoffman
SEARCH: *"Blitzscaling"*
FOLLOW: @ReidHoffman

Reid Hoffman is a man after my own heart. He loves people and he loves numbers. He studied cognitive science at Stanford and then studied philosophy at Oxford University. After joining Apple in 1994, Reid was one of the first employees of PayPal, running their operations until they got acquired by eBay. For his next venture he wanted to connect business executives "at scale" and so in 2002, he co-founded Linkedin, now the world's strongest professional network with over 500 million members. I have been fortunate to overhear two pieces of Reid Hoffman's advice during my own career, both have shaped the way that I think about people and numbers.

The first was at the tech conference SXSW in 2012 when Pinterest founder Ben Silberman was in conversation with Reid Hoffman and they were discussing the *"unfinished"* nature of Pinterest. Just by the bloggers lounge, chatting over a coffee, Reid said to Ben, *"If you are not embarrassed by the first version of your product, you launched it too late"*.

The second time was at a Linkedin event when Reid was encouraging the audience to focus on what was most meaningful, not just the most profitable. How do I do that in a way that will make my business stronger one executive asked? Hoffman replied, *"The value of your network is greater than the value of the services that you provide"*. I was so struck by that concept that I read all of Reid's books. I even spent every Friday morning for months reading every book that Reid was recommending to people on Twitter. It made me re-imagine how I thought about marketing: We should be building more *meaningful* relationships, not just more profitable or loyal ones.

#TENWORDS

GRACE HOPPER

"People are allergic to change, you must sell your idea".

Grace Hopper was a Navy Admiral and computer scientist who invented the first compiler in 1944, forever changing the way that we use computers. She had a jolly roger pirate flag on her desk to remind people that she was a rebel who got stuff done, and she had a backwards clock on her wall to show people that things don't always have to work just one way.

READ: *Grace Hopper* by Kurt Beyer
WATCH: Grace Hopper on Letterman
FOLLOW: @HopperAcademy

Grace Hopper is recognised as the mother of computer programming. She was a relentless trailblazer who created COBOL, the first complex computer language. After earning her PhD in mathematics from Yale in 1934 Grace served as a maths professor until 1943, when she quit her job to join the Women Accepted for Volunteer Emergency Service. The Navy sent her to Harvard to program one of the first ever electronic computers called the *Mark I*. Back then, calculations were done by large groups of people. Graces team used the *Mark I* to solve important problems for the war effort, including the implosion equation for the Manhattan Project.

Grace was always frustrated that programmers needed to use binary to program computers and have an advanced degree in mathematics. Grace thought it would be easier to just '*talk*' to a computer in English. Few people agreed with her or believed it was possible. It led her to create COBOL, the first universal computer language. It is because of Grace that today, it is possible for anyone to be able to code. Grace returned to the Navy in 1967 and continued to teach until she was 80. During those seminars and lectures, educating and inspiring the next generation of programmers, Grace made it her mission to remind her students that the most damaging phrase in the English language is *"We've always done it this way"*.

#TENWORDS

STEVE JOBS

"Provide compelling solutions that customers can **only** get from Apple".

Jobs is recognised for *doing* many things in business, but he liked to remind people that it was the things that he didn't do which made Apple great. *"I am more proud of the things we didn't do, than I am of what we did"*, he once said. As with many things in life, the key to success is knowing what to not get involved in.

READ: Jobs by Walter Isaacson.
WATCH: "Stamford Commencement Speech".
FOLLOW: In his footsteps.

When Steve Jobs returned to Apple as interim-CEO in 1997, the company he co-founded with Steve Wozniak was less than three months away from bankruptcy. The first thing he did was take a close look at Apple's marketing. Jobs soon concluded that the world's most emotional brand just *"wasn't very emotional anymore"*. Not only did people not know what Apple stood for, they didn't know what to buy either. When approached by a friend to recommend the right computer for their grandmother, Jobs had no idea what to suggest. There were over thirty-seven different product lines at the time and none of them seemed to have anything unique about them. Apple's marketing didn't have anything special or memorable about it either.

And so in what can only be described as the world's most successful whiteboard session, Jobs drew two intersecting lines on the wall with the words personal / professional on the X-axis and desktop / laptop on the Y-axis. He then told the team that from now on they would only be making four product lines. And to make sure that everyone understood which direction Apple was now going in, he also wrote these ten words on the wall. Shortly after, Jobs launched the *"Think Different"* campaign and just fourteen years later, having successfully escaped bankruptcy, Apple became recognised by Interbrand as the world's most valuable brand worth over $750 Billion.

#**TEN**WORDS

STEVE JOBS

"People don't know what they want until you show them".

Steve Jobs is simply the greatest CEO of all-time. Not just because of the global hype he generated, or the revenue he grew, but because of the *"reality distortion field"* he created which [inspired / forced] Apple employees to change the technology industry not just once, but three times (Mac, iPod+iTunes, iPhone).

READ: Think Simple by Ken Segall.
WATCH: The movie "Jobs" by Aaron Sorkin.
FOLLOW: Guy Kawasaki (Apple's first evangelist).

Steve Jobs wasn't just the world's greatest CEO, he was the world's best product marketer. He is also revered for arrogantly refusing to conduct consumer research or focus groups and these ten words have shaped the way that many business leaders now think about consumer research. Over one hundred years earlier, another controversial CEO called Henry Ford also became a business icon for thinking differently. The charismatic founder of Ford Motors allegedly made similar remarks to Jobs proclaiming, *"If I'd have asked people what they wanted, they would have said 'Faster horses!'"*.

Despite the fact that both these statements grace the pages of countless business books, neither of them are true. If you examine the evidence that Apple provided to the court when they sued Samsung in 2011 for various iPhone patent infringements, you'd discover that there was enough paperwork to take out a small rainforest. Apple knew more about Samsung than Samsung did. It wasn't that Steve Jobs didn't do research, it was that he didn't want anyone to know what he was doing. And with regard to the *"faster horses"*, there is no evidence of Henry Ford ever saying those words. What he actually said was less quotable but far more important, *"If there is any one secret of success, it lies in the ability to get the other person's point of view, and see things from that person's angle as well as your own."*

#TENWORDS

KATHERINE JOHNSON

"If you attack the problem properly, you'll get the answer".

Katherine Johnson is one of the most important mathematicians in the history of space travel. In 1952, she discovered that Langley Research Centre with the National Advisory Committee for Aeronautics (NACA) were looking to recruit mathematically-able African-American women. A year later, she began work there as a research mathematician with a team of women who Katherine remembers as *computers who wore skirts robotically processing data*".

"I found what I was looking for at Langley. This was what a research mathematician did. I went to work every day for 33 years happy. Never did I get up and say I don't want to go to work".

Katherine's passion for her job combined with her ability to solve problems that other people couldn't, eventually led her to calculate the flight path for Alan Shepard's first manned mission to the moon in 1961. Katherine also provided the highly complex calculations for propelling space capsules into orbit around the moon, sending landing units to and from the lunar surface, and calculating the trajectory for the Apollo 11 flight to the moon. Her later work included the Space Shuttle program and plans for a Mars mission. In her time at NASA, she co-authored 26 scientific papers and retired in 1986 after 33 years service. Not bad for a girl who was just *"obsessed with counting things"*.

"Luck is a combination of preparation and opportunity. If you're prepared and the opportunity comes up, it's your good fortune to have been in the right place at the right time and to have been prepared for the job." Katherine Johnson

READ: *Hidden Figures* by Margot Lee Shetterly
WATCH: *Hidden Figures* by Theodore Melfi
FOLLOW: @Stemettes

#**TEN**WORDS

CHARLES "CHUCK" JONES

"I have to think *as* Bugs Bunny, not *of* Bugs Bunny".

"An animator is an actor with a pencil".

Chuck Jones is one of the reasons I had such a happy childhood, wasting hundreds of hours watching the cartoons that he wrote. The perfect short-form storyteller, Chuck was the genius behind Bugs Bunny, Wile E. Coyote the Road Runner, Tom and Jerry and Daffy Duck. For his amazing work as a writer and animator, Chuck won three Academy Awards.

READ: *Chuck Amuck* by Chuck Jones
WATCH: Looney Tunes Cartoons!
FOLLOW: #LooneyTunes

Chuck Jones' father was a businessman, but much to the dismay of his wife, he was a very unsuccessful one. He was a dreamer who wanted to make some money and make a difference, but sadly each of his ventures failed. As with many clouds though, this one had a silver lining, because with each new venture came new stationery. But this wasn't any new stationery, because Chuck's father only bought stationery made from the highest quality paper. "*Image is everything!*" he proclaimed at the start of each new venture. Sadly, not enough people were "*impressed*" and the stacks of luxury paper and fine pencils were passed down to young Chuck each time the business closed down. As the beneficiary of said stationery, Chuck thrived. He spent every waking hour drawing and used up the stationery as fast as he could. He never worried about rationing his supplies, because his father joked that a new set of defunct stationery would probably arrive on Chuck's desk soon anyway. One day at school, Chuck's art teacher told the class that they each had 100,000 bad drawings in them to get past before they would ever draw anything useful. Chuck used this as fuel to fire his artistic ambitions and estimated he had done 200,000 bad drawings already. Chuck is now remembered as one of the greatest cartoonists and storytellers of all-time, thanks to his father who unwittingly turned his own miserable failures into joy for millions of cartoon lovers around the world.

#**TEN**WORDS

CHARLES "CHUCK" JONES

Rules For Wile. E. Coyote

1. The Road Runner cannot harm the Coyote except by going "beep beep"

2. No outside force can harm the Coyote — only his own ineptitude or the failure of Acme products.

3. The Coyote could stop anytime — if he were not a fanatic. (Repeat: "A fanatic is one who redoubles his effort when he has forgotten his aim." — George Santayana)."

4. No dialogue ever, except "beep-beep!"

5. The Road Runner must stay on the road — otherwise, logically, he would not be called Road Runner.

6. All action must be confined to the natural environment of the two characters — the southwest American desert.

7. All materials tools, weapons, or mechanical conveniences must be obtained from the Acme Corporation.

8. Whenever possible, make gravity the Coyote's greatest enemy.

9. The Coyote is always more humiliated than harmed by his failures.

#TENWORDS

MICHAEL JORDAN

"I'm happy we won five championships. But I want six".

Jordan's motivation for winning is summed up best in his most famous TV ad: "I've missed more than 9,000 shots in my career. I've lost almost 300 games. 26 times I've been trusted to take the game winning shot and missed. I've failed over and over and over in my life. And *that* is why I succeed". During his 15-year career MJ not only helped take the NBA from a top 5 American sport to a multi-billion dollar global franchise, but he built his own billion dollar brand in the process. The Jordan brand is now worth over $3 billion.

READ: *Michael Jordan: The Life* by Roland Lazenby
WATCH: *1997 NBA Finals Game 5*
FOLLOW: @ChicagoBulls

It is the attitude behind these ten words that drove Michael Jordan to become the greatest basketball player of all-time. Not too long ago a pair of Nike Air Jordan XII's sold for $100,000. The shoes were bought by an anonymous bidder, breaking the record for the most money ever paid for a pair of sneakers. The reason these shoes were so special was that Michael Jordan wore them for game 5 of the 1997 NBA finals, a game regarded by many basketball fans (including me) as the greatest performance by a single player in NBA history. Not because he had a high scoring game (he scored 38), but because of *how* he played. Jordan had the flu and this wasn't any regular man flu. This was a *"debilitating-throwing-up-haven't-slept-for-two-days"* kind of flu. Jordan played in 5-minute bursts often needing to be helped off the court by his team mate Scottie Pippen. Despite being sick, 23 still carried his Chicago Bulls to a close win in the final seconds, and onto their 5th championship.

I'll never forget watching the Bulls win that championship and noticing Jordan's teammates celebrating with champagne and holding up five fingers to signify their 5th championship. MJ was different. When the cameras panned across to Jordan he was holding up six. This summed up everything about the mindset of greatest ball player the game had ever seen. While everyone else was caught up in the moment, Jordan was already thinking about what was next.

#TENWORDS

TRAVIS KALANICK

"Push a button and a car arrives in five minutes".

One cold December evening back in 2008, Travis Kalanick was stuck on a street corner in Paris with his friend Garrett Camp. It was just after 3am and had started to snow, but despite it being the centre of Paris, there were no taxis to be found anywhere. Both of them were very successful tech entrepreneurs having both recently sold their companies*, so they started doing what tech entrepreneurs do best ~ they started jamming on new ideas while they were waiting for a ride. Kalanick's idea of pushing a button so that a car arrives in five minutes seems obvious today, but back then it had never been done before. Nobody was talking about a "sharing (or collaborative) economy" and it would be a few more years before entrepreneurs started to drop "disruption" into every sentence.

These ten words gave birth to Uber, the $65 billion taxi company which is currently the fastest growing startup and the world's most valuable startup. Travis's vision is to become a monopoly. Part of this is driven by his ego and his ambition, but he also has a deeper purpose that many people don't talk about. Travis told me at the Dreamforce conference in 2015 that if 70% of the cars in large cities were Ubers, the average person might gain an hour in their day from not being stuck in traffic. And that, simply, is where Uber's ten word mission came from. *"Provide transportation as reliable as running water. Everywhere. For everyone".*

Travis believes that there is nothing democratic about building a company, especially one that operates in a tough industry with strong traditions. In a democracy, you often win 51-49. If you want to build the next Uber-of-whatever, you need a different philosophy. According to Kalanick, you need to destroy the competition and "win 98-2", an attitude which caused his eventual downfall when he was forced to resign as Uber's CEO in mid-2017.

READ: Travis Kalanick interview in Vanity Fair.
WATCH: Travis Kalanick on TWiST, Episode #180
FOLLOW: @TravisK

*In 2007 Travis Kalanick sold Red Swoosh for $19M to Akamai Technologies and Garrett Camp sold StumbleUpon to eBay for $75M.

#**TEN**WORDS

KEVIN KELLY

"The future happens very slowly and then all at once".

Kevin Kelly wrote *"The Inevitable"*. It was one of the best books I read in 2016 about the twelve technological forces that are most likely to shape our future. In it, he tells the story of how he confronted Google co-founder Larry Page in 2002, challenging him about how he expected to make any money building a search engine. Larry replied, *"We're really making an AI"*. Fifteen years later, Google is now telling everyone they are an *"AI first company"*. Kevin Kelly noticed it first.

READ: *The Inevitable* by Kevin Kelly
WATCH: ALL of Kevin Kelly's TED Talks
FOLLOW: @Wired

Kevin Kelly is the reason that so many people get seduced by new technologies and the possibilities they promise. As the founder of Wired magazine, Kevin has made it his mission to showcase new innovations in the tech world and comment on what they mean to us. Innovation is an interesting word but it was Kevin Kelly who taught me what it really meant. The terms innovation or disruption are often used interchangeably, despite being quite different. Innovation is simply doing something that already exists a bit faster than everyone else. Disruption, on the other hand is inventing a new thing that makes the old thing obsolete. Big difference. Uber, for example is *innovative* (the tech already existed), but a cognitive technology like IBM's Watson is a *disruptive* technology (as it is making current technologies in healthcare, commerce and marketing obsolete).

What I love most about Kevin though is that despite evangelising new technologies, he believes that moving faster isn't always better. Despite the promise that emerging tech like AR, VR and AI bring, Kevin insists that we should not get too seduced by shiny new things. *"There is no business case for innovation"*, Kevin said recently on a podcast with marketer Mitch Joel, *"what people should really do is perfect what they know"*. In other words, focus on the fundamentals of your business before investing in unproven new technologies. Wise words.

#TENWORDS

JAN KOUM

"I want to do one thing, and do it well".

When Whatsapp co-founder Jan Koum agreed for Facebook to acquire his five-year old company for US$19 billion in 2014, he asked if he could sign the paperwork on the steps of the welfare office where he used to collect his food stamps. Jan was raised in a rural community in the Ukraine, in a house with no hot water or electricity. His school didn't even have an inside bathroom, despite it being near Kiev where the temperatures would drop to -20°C. When Jan's family moved to the US seeking the American dream, his mother packed their suitcases with school supplies to save money. As a young immigrant, Koum and his mother had to rely on food stamps, and so in a poignant tribute to his humble past, he chose to sign the deal with Facebook at the same welfare office in Mountain View where he used to queue to get food stamps. Today Jan is worth almost $9 billion and the office where Whatsapp serves its 700 million users is located only a few blocks away.

Koum and Acton cared so deeply about user privacy from the beginning that they said, "*We want to know as little about our users as possible. We're not advertisement-driven so we don't need personal databases*". When challenged about a marketing strategy they had a similarly unique perspective: "*Marketing and press kicks up dust. It gets in your eye, and then you're not focusing on the product*."

Jan Koum and Brian Acton co-founded Whatsapp in 2009 with one mission and six words: They wanted to "*do one thing well*" and agreed that the app must have "*no ads, no games, no gimmicks*". Just two years earlier they were refused jobs at Facebook after they returned from a trip to South America where they came up with the idea for a messaging app, letting people set status updates on their phones. Funny how things turn out when you focus on just one thing.

READ: *On Jan Koum* (Business Insider, May 2017)
WATCH: *From 0 – 1 Bn Users* : Startup Grind Conference
LISTEN: *Jan Koum and David Rowan* (DLD14)

#**TEN**WORDS

JEFF KOONS

"I try to be a truthful artist. I'm a messenger".

"Art is obsolete now. New technologies are taking over. A photographer just working for an advertising company has a platform to be much more politically effective in the world than an artist". Jeff Koons

READ: *Now* by Jeff Koons
WATCH: *Imagine: Jeff Koons* (BBC)
FOLLOW: @JeffKoons

Jeff Koons is the world's most commercially successful living artist. Critics are sharply divided in their views of Koons. Some view his work as pioneering and of major art-historical importance. Others dismiss his work as kitsch crass, based on cynical self-merchandising originating from a carefully managed production process. Koons is more of a curator than a traditional artist. It's easy to see why the art world doesn't like him very much. Koons is just the idea's person and doesn't actually make much of his own art personally. He said, *"I'm not physically involved in the production. I don't have the necessary abilities, so I go to the top people"*.

Koons has stated that there are no hidden or profound meanings in his works. He just sees himself simply as a messenger who uses his art to connect people to each other. It's a heart-breakingly sad story, but the only reason Koons created his infamous balloon puppy was in the hope that his estranged son would see it. Koons lost a messy custody battle after his marriage in 1991 to Ilona Stellar, an Italian porn star and politician. He fought for years, losing most of his possessions to pay for legal fees to see his son, but sadly lost the case and was prevented from interacting with him. So in an effort to communicate with his son Ludwig from afar, he made a giant balloon puppy that he thought his son might like. That Balloon Dog sold at Christie's for $58.4M in 2013. He still hasn't seen Ludwig.

#**TEN**WORDS

JEFF KOONS

On November 12, 2013, Koons's Balloon Dog (Orange) sold at Christie's Post-War and Contemporary Art Evening Sale in New York City for US$58.4 million, above its high US$55 million estimate, becoming the most expensive work by a living artist sold at auction.

#TENWORDS

JOHN F. KENNEDY

"Efforts and courage are not enough without purpose and direction".

"All great and honourable actions are accompanied with great difficulties". John F. Kennedy. 35th President of the United States of America, the youngest president elected, the first Catholic president and Storyteller-in-Chief.

When most politicians are elected into office, they talk about improving healthcare, cutting taxes and raising the standards of our schools. All important stuff. But stuff that is often based upon making marginal improvements on what went before. But when John F. Kennedy got elected president of the United States in 1960 he wasn't interested in just marginally improving the US economy. He wanted to do something bigger. He wanted to go to the moon.

JFK may have been motivated as much by a desire to beat the Russians as he was to conquer a new frontier, but promising a manned moon landing within a decade was still a bold move by a bold president. So, when Kennedy made his *"moon speech"* at Rice University during a trip to dedicate NASA's new manned Spacecraft Center, his words led him to be hailed as a space visionary. In what I think is a more evocative speech than his infamous *"ask not what your country can do for you"* inauguration speech, Kennedy spoke about knowledge, technology and the human spirit, more eloquently than perhaps anyone before or since him.

"But why, some say, the Moon? Why choose this as our goal? And they may well ask, why climb the highest mountain? Why, 35 years ago, fly the Atlantic? We choose to go to the Moon! We choose to go to the Moon in this decade and do the other things, not because they are easy, but because they are hard".

READ: JFK's *"Moon" Speech* (12th September 1962)
WATCH: *JFK: A Documentary* by Jack Anderson
LISTEN: *JFK's Inauguration Speech* (1961)

#**TEN**WORDS

JOHN F. KENNEDY

Was the 1960 presidential TV debate between Kennedy and Nixon a triumph of style over substance?

As the first ever televised debate, much has been written about the impact of the presidential debate in 1960, and how JFK presented himself better on screen and relied upon media friendly sound bites to win over the short attention spans of the American population. As is often the case, marketers and Mad Men at the time used whatever metrics they could to try and sell the promise of this new media, much like the conversations that exist around digital v traditional media today. And just like today, most of the metrics used in making those arguments were either wrong or taken out of context. According to the Mad Men, for example, people watching on television thought JFK won, while people listening on the radio gave the edge to Nixon. More than 70 million people watched on TV, out of a population of roughly 110 million U.S. adults, but the TV viewing figures were only based on a survey of 2,100 respondents - of whom only 282 listened on the radio. Only 178 of them expressed an opinion on who won the debate. "*Lies. Damned lies. And statistics*" as Twain might say.

Others thought the debate was a triumph of style over substance when in fact Ted Sorensen, JFK's speechwriter, argued in a 2010 New York Times op-ed that "*there was far more substance and nuance in that first debate than in what now passes for political debate in our commercialized, sound-bite Twitter-fied culture, in which extremist rhetoric requires presidents to respond to outrageous claims.*" Ted went on to say that despite the promise of headline making sound bites, two minutes of big ideas squashed into short sentences is no time at all to give an important answer. All you can do is educate the audience.

#**TEN**WORDS

HEDY LAMAR

"Films have a certain place in time. Technology is forever".

"My father made me understand that I must make my own decisions, mold my own character, think my own thoughts".
Hedy Lamar

READ: *Hedy's Folly* by Richard Rhodes
WATCH: *Samson and Delilah* featuring Hedy Lamar
FOLLOW: @HedyLamarr

Hedy Lamar was not your typical movie star. Despite having a star on the Hollywood Hall of Fame and appearing in movies alongside Clark Gable, Spencer Tracy and Jimmy Stewart, she also co-invented the technology behind *"frequency-hopping spread spectrum communication"*. Hedy Lamar was a beautifully intelligent genius.

During World War II, she learned that radio-controlled torpedoes, which could be important in the naval war, could easily be jammed, thereby causing the torpedo to go off course. With the knowledge she *"acquired"* from overhearing trade secrets over dinner from her first husband (the Chairman of a leading Austrian weapons manufacturer), she came up with the idea of creating a frequency-hopping signal that could not be tracked or jammed. She contacted her friend, composer and pianist George Antheil, to help her develop a device for doing that, and he succeeded by synchronizing a miniaturized player-piano mechanism with radio signals. They drafted designs for the frequency-hopping system which they patented. Her work has since been developed widely and is now the foundation for GPS, Wi-Fi and Bluetooth. As a result of her pioneering work, she was inducted into the National Inventors Hall of Fame in 2014. If ever there was a person who epitomised what is possible when you live your life at the intersection of art and science it was Hedy Lamar.

#TENWORDS

JOHN LASSETER

"Art challenges the technology and the technology inspires the art".

"Your voice is worthwhile. Have faith in it". John Lasseter

In 1983 John and his wife moved to the San Francisco Bay Area, where John got a job at the Lucasfilm's computer division, a group tasked with developing computer technology for the film industry. In 1986 some guy called Steve Jobs decided that he wanted to re-invent the animated movie industry and bought the division for $10 million, establishing Pixar. Over the next few years, Jobs would invest $50 million to stop Pixar running out of money, determined that Pixar would disrupt other movie studios like Disney. The first time John met Jobs they discussed what Pixar's first project should be. Lasseter pitched the idea for a short film called *Tin Toy*. John described the story and presented some beautiful storyboard illustrations, but it was clear that Steve's head was somewhere else. He was picturing what the future might look like for Pixar. After a few moments, he asked John to do something. It was the only time Steve ever asked John to do anything,

"John, make it great".

Those four words changed everything. *Tin Toy* went on to win the Academy Award for Best Animated Short Picture, re-defining the way that art and technology would co-exist. Steve, John and Ed Catmull transformed that small Lucasfilm division into an animation studio and as Jobs had predicted, Pixar went on to disrupt Disney so dramatically that they were forced to buy them. For $7.4Bn!

READ: *Creativity Inc* by Ed Catmull
WATCH: *The Pixar Story* by Leslie Iwerks
FOLLOW: @Pixar

#**TEN**WORDS

The average person sees 100,000 digital words each day.

Ten words storytellers can use to make a memorable impact:

Now

Amazing

Suddenly

Announcing

Sensational

Remarkable

Revolutionary

Challenge

Miracle

Magic

@MATTHEW**LUHN**
PIXAR SCRIPTWRITER (TOY STORY, INSIDE OUT, WALL-E)

#TENWORDS

ESTÉE LAUDER

"I never dreamed of success. I worked hard for it".

"I have never worked a day in my life without selling. If I believe in something, I sell it, and I sell it hard".

Estée Lauder was the only woman on TIME magazine's list of the 20 most influential business geniuses of the 20th century. She built a $4 billion empire, which started by taking her uncle's homemade skin cream, *"branding"* it and selling it to her hairdresser.

READ: *Estée: A Success Story* by Estée Lauder
WATCH: Estée Lauder's YouTube Channel
FOLLOW: @EsteeLauder

Estée Lauder has been voted one of the most influential marketers of all-time. She was a great marketer, re-branding generic skin care products that her uncle made in his chemist, but she was an even better sales woman. Many marketers talk about their hopes, dreams and visions for the future, but not Estée Lauder. She talked about nothing but hard work, an ethic she instilled into her sales. *"If you don't sell, it's not the product that's wrong it's you".*

It would be easy to argue against that statement if the product was average, but in Lauder's case, her product was the best in the category. Her vision was that *"3 minutes is all beauty should ever take"*, because women, no matter how busy they were, could always afford to look and feel good. Her philosophy of short beauty regimes also matched her philosophy of short marketing campaigns. Long before influencer marketing was popular, Estée Lauder was proclaiming, *"Influencers make the brand"*. It sounds obvious today, but in 1947 this was revolutionary. She started the company with just four products and gave small samples of them to her famous friends and acquaintances, wanting her brand in the hands of people who were known for having the best. It paid off. Within two years Saks Fifth Avenue in New York became the first Estée Lauder counter in the world and the cosmetics industry would be changed forever.

#TENWORDS

JOHN LENNON

"The more I see the less I know for sure".

"It ain't what you don't know that gets you into trouble. It's what you know for sure that just ain't so". Mark Twain inspired John Lennon's *ten words*.

READ: *In His Own Write* by John Lennon
WATCH: *Eight Days A Week* by Ron Howard
FOLLOW: @TheBeatles

John Lennon was one of the great storytellers and songwriters of modern times. I grew up with The Beatles and loved reading the album notes from my parent's original LP's and learning the lyrics. I remember being obsessed with the song lengths as I tried to figure out what would fit onto my TDK C-90 cassette tapes, and worked out that the average Beatles song was 2 minutes 25 seconds long. Compare that to a modern band like Coldplay and most songs approach 5 minutes. John Lennon understood how to put powerful words into short songs with small sentences. And the best sentence he ever wrote? *"That's easy"*, he replied when asked by a journalist from Rolling Stone, *"All you need is love"*.

The first time I stepped foot in a Red Bull office they were playing that exact song. I remember it because they also had a slogan on the wall next to where their social team sat which read, *"50% of people use social media to waste time - so let's give them some cool shit to do when they get there"*. I like to think that Red Bull were inspired by the great John Lennon quote, *"Time you enjoy wasting is not wasted time"*. Lennon enjoyed wasting a lot of time in between writing some of the world's finest (and shortest) songs. Apparently, it was in one of those moments of wasteful reflection that he dropped his ten words of wisdom. A great reminder for all of us to stay curious...

#TENWORDS

ABRAHAM LINCOLN

"I destroy my enemies when I make them my friends".

"The things I want to know are in books; my best friend is the man who'll get me a book I ain't read". Abraham Lincoln

READ: *Lincoln the Unknown* by Dale Carnegie
WATCH: *Lincoln* by Steven Spielberg
FOLLOW: @Mr_Lincoln

Lincoln was undoubtedly one of the greatest communicators of all-time. His words entertain, educate, and inspire audiences to this day, but it took a lot of hard work for him to end up where he did. With only one year of formal schooling, Lincoln consciously cultivated his mastery of language and expression. As a young boy he would practice public speaking by gathering his friends together and stepping onto a stump to address them. During his days as a lawyer in Illinois, Lincoln would frequently meet up with friends at a tavern and engage in story-telling contests. He also learned valuable lessons in rhetoric by studying Shakespeare and often stayed up into the early hours to read Webster's dictionary on his porch by candlelight, much to the dismay of his wife.

But like all great orators, Lincolns' speaking success was not attributed to his vocabulary, but his preparation. *"Give me six hours to chop down a tree and I will spend the first four sharpening the axe"*, he once said. Lincoln certainly did his fair share of axe sharpening, preparing words for every occasion, so when he was called upon *"to make a few appropriate remarks"* before the troops on Thursday 19th November 1863, he knew exactly what to say. Taking just two minutes to share 270 carefully chosen words, Lincoln made a speech which would never be forgotten*. Proof, as if it were needed, that the best speeches are short, and contain big ideas, small words and short sentences.

* The Gettysburg Address, delivered during the American Civil War in 1863 is one of the greatest speeches of all-time.

#TENWORDS

ADA LOVELACE

"I am not a mathematician, I am a *Poetical Scientist*".

Ada Lovelace was the original computer *"scientist"*. She was the first person to create a computer program and wrote one of the most famous documents in computer history. Her program was inspired by the punch cards used in mechanical looms which would go on to form the basis of IBM's core business in the early 19th century.

READ: *The Analytical Engine* (Translated by A.L.)
WATCH: *Conceiving Ada* by Lynn Hershman-Leeson
FOLLOW: Ada Lovelace Day (2nd Tuesday in October)

When Ada Lovelace first saw the Difference Engine in 1833, she became obsessed. It had been built by the early computing pioneer Charles Babbage and was basically a gigantic, gear-filled mechanical calculator. Arranging to meet him as soon as could, she persuaded him to work with her. In her pitch, Ada described herself as a *"Poetical Scientist"*. I love that term. Long before we were talking about *"technology"*, Ada was talking about the intersection of humanity and science and the importance of understanding patterns and numbers. Like many of the most influential scientists who came before and after her, she saw art in numbers and was convinced that science was as much a discipline of the heart as it was of the head. Ada's father was the famed poet Lord Byron.

1833 was a momentous year in science not just because of Ada's achievements, but because attitudes like hers were permeating scientific groups and Royal societies. Challenged by attitudes like Ada's, a group from Cambridge University called *The British Association for the Advancement of Science* called a meeting and decided that they needed to stop referring to themselves as *"natural philosophers"*. The man leading the debate was not a science professor. He was the poet Samuel Taylor Coleridge. "*If 'philosophers' is taken to be too wide and lofty a term, then, by analogy with 'artist,' we may form 'scientist.'*" This was the first time the word scientist was uttered in public.

#TENWORDS

JACK MA

"I am a blind man riding on a blind tiger".

In just one and a half decades, Jack Ma, a man from modest beginnings who started out as an English teacher, founded and built Alibaba into one of the world's largest companies, an e-commerce empire on which hundreds of millions of Chinese consumers depend. Alibaba's $25 billion IPO in 2014 was the largest global IPO ever.

READ: *Never Give Up* by Jack Ma
WATCH: Jack Ma at Davos 2017
FOLLOW: $BABA (NYSE)

When KFC first arrived in China, 24 people went for a job. 23 people were successful. Jack Ma wasn't. Determined not to give up, he kept applying and got a job as a server at a branch of KFC in his hometown of Hangzhou. Jack's next plan was to go to college, but he failed the entrance exam. Three times. Once he had ruled out college, Jack applied for 30 different jobs and got rejected. He even went for a job with the police and they said, *"You're no good"*.

Realising that nobody wanted to give him a job, Jack decided to employ himself. He founded Alibaba in 1998 but was soon met with even more obstacles. The brand did not turn a profit for the first three years, and Jack had to get creative. One of the company's main challenges was that it had no way to do payments, and no banks would work with him, so Jack did what any other entrepreneur would do, he decided to start his own payment program called Alipay. The program transfers payments of different currencies between international buyers and sellers. Many of his advisors at the time told him, *"This is the stupidest idea you've ever had"*. Jack didn't care if it was stupid as long as people could use it. Jack refused to give up. Today, 800 million people use Alipay and Alibaba is the world's largest e-commerce company valued at $200 billion. And in what now seems like a beautifully act of karma, in 2016 Jack bought a stake in Yum Brands, the holding group for KFC.

#TENWORDS

JACK MA

"I am a very simple guy, I am not smart. Everyone thinks that Jack Ma is a very smart guy.

I might have a smart face but I've got very stupid brains,,.

虎

#**TEN**WORDS

JOHN MACKEY

"Businesses should view people not as resources but as sources".

"If you don't have a cause you should get one".

John Mackey, the co-founder of Wholefoods is passionate about building trust between management and employees. He made Whole Foods one of the first companies in the world to disclose the annual salaries of all its employees in a 'salary book', which was made available at all its locations. This created a culture of trust and openness at the company.

READ: *Conscious Capitalism* by John Mackey
WATCH: Darden Leadership Series with John Mackey
FOLLOW: @Wholefoods

In 1978, a twenty-five year old college dropout called John Mackey decided that he wanted to re-invent the grocery business. So along with his friend Rene Lawson Hardy he borrowed $45,000 from family and friends to open the doors of a small natural foods store called SaferWay, in Austin, Texas. The business did well but it wasn't long before the pair got booted out of their apartment for storing food products there. Living on a shoestring, but believing in their mission, they decided to simply live at their store instead. Since the building was "zoned" as a commercial property, there was no shower, but being the resourceful entrepreneurs that they were, they bathed in their Hobart dishwasher, which had an attached water hose. Within two years they merged with the Clarksville Natural Grocery and established the first Whole Foods Market on September 20, 1980. The rest, as they say, is history.

"Purpose is something we can never take for granted; the moment we do, it starts to be forgotten and soon disappears. It has to be at the forefront of consciousness (and therefore decision making) literally all the time".

Today, Whole Foods Market, Inc. is the largest natural-foods grocer in the United States and has 431 stores globally with revenues approaching $13 billion. Whole Foods also donate a substantial 5% of after-tax profits to not-for-profit organizations.

JOHN MACKEY

CONSCIOUS CAPITALISM
by John Mackey

The ten words I chose to represent Mackey for this book stem from the phrase *Conscious Capitalism* which he coined in his book of the same name published in 2014. It is a great read and explains how capitalism has been under attack for a long time. This is partly down to the fact that too many businesses have operated with a low level of consciousness about their true purpose and overall impact on the world. Some of the attacks have not been without substance when you consider that, according to the Institute for Policy Studies, the ratio between CEO pay and average pay increased from 42:1 in 1980 to 325:1 in 2010. If an average worker gets paid £50,000, this is equivalent to a CEO receiving £16.2m! Combine this with the short sighted obsession of many businesses to drive sales instead of increasing customer value, and it is not surprising that the reputation of business has suffered. Many corporations exist without a conscience and therefore have been tagged as greedy, selfish, exploitative and untrustworthy.

Capitalism has also done many great things though. It has created an environment of creativity and innovation that allows every one of us an unprecedented level of access to information. **It's easy to forget that ordinary people today have access to virtually limitless information on any subject, any time, any place, instantly at almost zero cost. This is a privilege that the richest billionaire in the world did not have access to twenty years ago.** This is why in his book, John Mackey holds entrepreneurs in such high regard,

"Entrepreneurs are the true heroes in a free enterprise economy, driving progress in business, society, and the world. They solve problems by creatively envisioning different ways the world could and should be. With their imagination, creativity, passion, and energy, they are the greatest curators of widespread change in the world. They are able to see new possibilities and enrich the lives of others by creating things that never existed before".

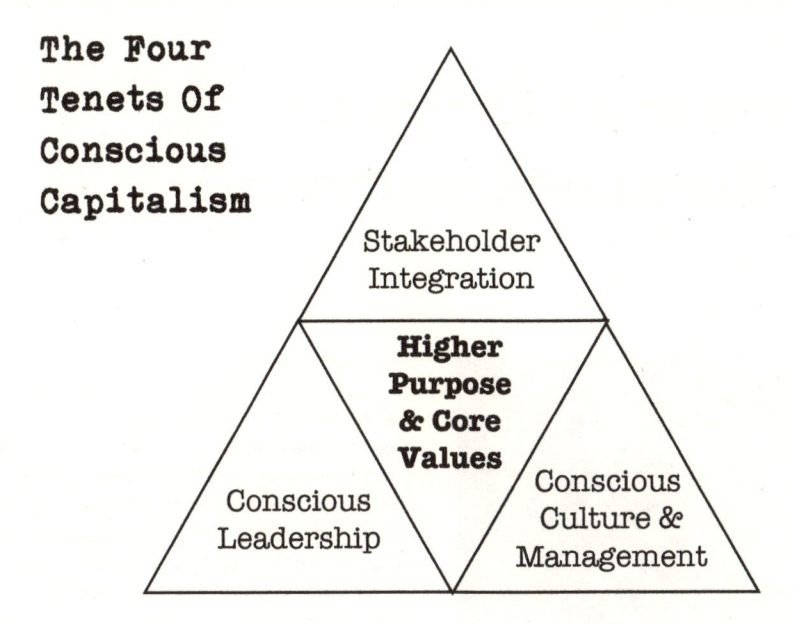

#**TEN**WORDS

JOHN MACKEY

The Four Tenets Of Conscious Capitalism

- Stakeholder Integration
- **Higher Purpose & Core Values**
- Conscious Leadership
- Conscious Culture & Management

Businesses have a much broader impact on the world when they are based on a higher purpose that goes beyond just generating profits and creating shareholder value. *"Purpose"* is the reason a company exists. Purpose driven companies ask questions such as: Why does our business exist? Why does it need to exist? What core values animate the enterprise and unite all of our shareholders?

ARE PURPOSE DRIVEN BRANDS MORE SUCCESSFUL?

According to research by John Mackey and his *'thought partner'* Prof. Raj Sisodia, *"conscious"* firms outperformed the overall stock market by 10.5:1 over a fifteen-year period, delivering more than 1,600% total returns when the market was up just over 150% in the same period. The basis for this was a sample of 28 companies which Sisodia identified as purpose-driven brands. The 18 publicly traded companies out of the 28 that they picked outperformed the S&P500 index by 10.5 from 1996-2011. The conclusion of their research? Conscious companies treat their stakeholders better.

#TENWORDS

JOHN C. MAXWELL

"People will always sum up your life in one sentence".

John C. Maxwell has written seventy-one books and sold over 19 million copies. When I met John he told me that he campaigned for his book *"The 360° Leader"* to be called *"Leading From The Middle of The Pack: Follow Me I'm Right Behind You"*, but the publisher said it wasn't commercial enough. He offered to give me the title if I wanted to use it! Sounds like the perfect title for a marketing leadership book.

READ: *Today Matters* by John C. Maxwell
WATCH: John's 5 Levels of Leadership Keynote
FOLLOW: @JohnCMaxwell

I have read many of the seventy-one books that John C. Maxwell has written, which makes him just about the closest thing I have ever had to a mentor. I first met John in 2005 when I learned that he was hosting a leadership conference in Bradford. I was astonished to learn that his speaking fee was £100,000 but he might be willing to reduce it to £50,000 if the dates coincided with another European conference he was already speaking at. What could anybody possibly say that would be worth paying them £100,000 for one day of their time? So, along with 1,000 other "business leaders", I paid my £50 and got there early to find a seat near the front. I wasn't disappointed.

John spoke over five sessions that day with each one lasting *exactly* 59 minutes. The event organisers set up a nice stage set with a huge screen, spotlights and a lectern. He didn't need them. The best speakers never do. And so with no notes, no prompter and no PowerPoint or videos to stimulate our attention, John kept the audience on the edge of their seat all day. It was an incredible performance and the first time that I truly understood that one perfectly placed piece of advice could save an organisation millions. Whatever Jon got paid and however much people paid to be there was worth it. He said many great things that day (I took 17 pages of notes!) but it was John's challenge to each of us to find our own *"one sentence"* that I will never forget.

#**TEN**WORDS

LEE ALEXANDER McQUEEN

"If it doesn't change the industry I'm not doing it".

McQueen used to describe fashion as *"your secret armour"*. Leaders such as Obama, Tom Ford and Zuckerberg wear the same thing every day. Putting on their *armour (as they also describe it)* prepares them for whatever that day throws at them. In the early days of building his brand, Lee Alexander McQueen had no money but rather than buy food, he used his unemployment benefit money to buy fabric that made the clothes that represented his armour.

READ: *Alexander McQueen* by Claire Wilcox
WATCH: Any McQueen interview on YouTube
FOLLOW: @AlexanderMcQueen

How different would our jobs be if we lived by these ten words? I first heard McQueen drop them into an interview during London Fashion Week a few years ago. He wasn't intending to make a provocative statement for headline purposes. This was no shallow Twitter-friendly soundbite. McQueen genuinely meant it, and he spent his entire career living by it. It was sadly a very short lived career, but as with all visionaries who are taken from us too soon, McQueen's fashion shows and collections have inspired a generation of creatives who are driven by more than personal success or financial gain.

McQueen's shows were like performance art. They weren't fashion shows. Every one of them made a statement and they relied on the audience's engagement. As a designer, he was unique in his ability to make his audience react emotionally to his presentations. McQueen once remarked, *"I don't want to do a cocktail party, I'd rather people left my shows and vomited"*. Consider any presentation you have ever given. How much of it do you think was remembered by your audience the next day? Or the following week? Scientists who research attention spans have suggested to me that it is between 5%-10%. We don't necessarily need to make people want to vomit each time we present, but I'm pretty sure that anyone who has ever seen a McQueen show still talks about it, and probably remembers a LOT more than 10%.

LEE ALEXANDER McQUEEN

#TENWORDS

#**TEN**WORDS

TAMARA MELLON

"Trust your instincts. People who are over educated become risk-averse ".

Tamara Mellon borrowed $150,000 from her father Tommy Yeardye (co-founder of Vidal Sassoon) to start Jimmy Choo. She lives by the mantra, *"I don't really care about gossip. I care about building great businesses"*.

Tamara Mellon had a privileged life growing up, but that didn't stop her thinking big. Beginning her career in fashion PR, she worked her contacts hard and soon secured a job as the accessories editor for British Vogue. It was there that she approached bespoke shoe designer Jimmy Choo with the idea of them launching a ready-to-wear shoe company together. You can read enough about her turbulent life on Wikipedia, but when you do, remember that Tamara battled to reach the top of her profession by following her gut feelings and trusting her instincts. To others in the fashion industry, many of her business decisions didn't make sense, but then again why would they, they didn't help found one of the world's most desired shoe brands or chose to pose naked for a magazine shoot. No, Tarama was not your average CEO. Understanding the power of celebrity, she was one of the first luxury brands to exploit the power of the red carpet by hand dying her shoes to the exact colour of the celebrities' dresses. She now practically 'owns' the shoe suite at the Oscars. When she first started out, luxury brands didn't give away much free stock, but against the advice of her investors, she chose to invest in A-lister "experiences" instead of expensive ads. It paid off. Jimmy Choo now has over 115 stores in 32 countries. Working on her next venture (a fast-fashion luxury brand inspired by H&M), Tamara is still trusting her instincts. Many think it will fail. Of course, it won't.

READ: *Tarama Mellon, Lunch with the FT.*
WATCH: *Talking Shoes With Jimmy Choo*
FOLLOW: @TamaraMellon

#TENWORDS

MARILYN MONROE

"It takes a smart brunette to play a dumb blonde".

"Wanting to be someone else is a waste of the person you are."
Marilyn Monroe

Marilyn Monroe lived a paradoxical life. She allowed herself to be typecast as the *dumb blonde* believing that's what her audience wanted, a role which made her Hollywood's highest paid actress for over a decade, but deep down she preferred to be the smart brunette. By day she enjoyed playing the comic *"dumb blonde"* in movies such as *Gentlemen Prefer Blondes* and *Some Like It Hot* but by night, she was the *"smart brunette"* who loved to spend hours flicking through the books in Pickwick's bookstore on Hollywood Boulevard. Marilyn spent many evenings searching for books that inspired her, so that she would remain inspired, reading them on set the following day. As a result of her many trips to Pickwick's, Marilyn's most treasured possessions were the 400 classic books in her library, many of them first editions.

Movie directors were often surprised that inbetween filming silly comedy scenes, she could be found at the back of the lot reading some serious poetry. It's hard to imagine how conflicted Marilyn must have been, loving the spotlight but desperately trying to stay true to herself. Legend has it that she lived by a ten word philosophy which helped her to stay positive, *"things fall apart so that better things can fall together"*. In the end, it is heartbreaking that she didn't *fall together* enough times, but she left us with some great films and some amazingly quotable sentences. Rest in peace Norma Jean.

READ: More poetry
WATCH: *Niagara* directed by Henry Hathaway (1953)
FOLLOW: @MarilynMonroe

#TEN WORDS

MARILYN MONROE

A WOMAN IS OFTEN MEASURED BY THE THINGS SHE CANNOT CONTROL. SHE IS MEASURED BY THE WAY HER BODY CURVES OR DOESN'T CURVE, BY WHERE SHE IS FLAT OR STRAIGHT OR ROUND. SHE IS MEASURED BY 36-24-36 AND INCHES AND AGES AND NUMBERS, BY ALL THE OUTSIDE THINGS THAT DON'T EVER ADD UP TO WHO SHE IS ON THE INSIDE. AND SO IF A WOMAN IS TO BE MEASURED, LET HER BE MEASURED BY THE THINGS SHE CAN CONTROL, BY WHO SHE IS AND WHO SHE IS TRYING TO BECOME. BECAUSE AS EVERY WOMAN KNOWS, MEASUREMENTS ARE ONLY STATISTICS. AND **STATISTICS LIE.**

Marilyn Monroe for Nike. A beautiful piece of copywriting, respectfully written by Nike based upon Marilyn's thoughts about self image and body confidence.

#TENWORDS

ELON MUSK

"I want to think about the future without being sad".

"My proceeds from the PayPal acquisition were $180 million. I put $100 million in SpaceX, $70m in Tesla, and $10m in Solar City. I had to borrow money for rent." Elon Musk

READ: *Elon Musk* by Ashlee Vance
WATCH: *Elon Musk* at TED (2017)
FOLLOW: Everyone @ElonMusk follows

Elon Musk doesn't want to be *"anyone's saviour"* but he is clearly driven by a higher purpose. He is famous for having visions that will change the world, but he wants to do more than talk about them, he wants to make them a reality. I'll never forget watching Chris Anderson interview him at TED in 2017 and watching how totally baffled Chris was by many of Elon's answers. Chris is used to interviewing people who have changed the world in some way, but Chris appeared genuinely baffled at how Elon's mind worked. But then again, if you are simultaneously building the world's largest electric car manufacturer, while also working on driverless vehicles, building a battery plant, solar cities, hyper-loops, subterranean transport systems, trying to colonise Mars and protecting mankind from "bad AI", then you are clearly not dealing with a rational person.

"Optimism, pessimism, fuck that; we're going to make it happen".

Many people call Elon's projects *"moonshots"*, but he doesn't think of them as moonshots at all. He just feels like it is his responsibility to address these problems, because solutions are not inevitable. I encourage you to watch Elon's TED interview because as you listen to Musk's stories, you will begin to understand what makes him tick. It might even inspire you to think a bit bigger and be *"less sad"* about our future.

#**TEN**WORDS

ELON MUSK

TIME Magazine voted Elon Musk one of the 100 most influential people of all time

#TENWORDS

BLAKE MYCOSKIE

"Stories are the most primitive and purest form of communication".

"If you organize your life around your passion, you can turn your passion into your story and then turn your story into something bigger ~ something that matters".
Blake Mycoskie, Founder of TOMS*

*TOMS is a "philanthropic retailer", born from a social mission: to outfit needy children with shoes.

READ: *Start Something That Matters*
SUBSCRIBE: TOMS Email Newsletter
FOLLOW: @BlakeMycoskie | @TOMS

Blake Mycoskie has built a billion dollar business by telling stories about three little words. Three little words which have connected with a generation of customers on such a deep level that they reinvented the way that many people think about philanthropy. "Millennials" (yes, I used the "M" word) who may have previously just given spare change to a homeless person and sponsored their friend for a few pounds, are now regularly paying over-the-odds prices for products, knowing that each sale will gift a similar product to a child in need. It turns a simple sale into an empowering process that turns the buyer into mini-philanthropists. As a result TOMS (named after "TOMorrowS shoes) have built one of the strongest communities of social and retail activists on social media. And the three words that refer to this world-changing business model? *"One-for-One"*.

Those three little words encapsulate a retail model so powerful that they have inspired several other brands to copy it. The TOMS story begins when Blake was a marketing executive looking for a startup idea to make his fortune. While on a trip to Argentina in 2006 he came across alpargata's, the cheaply made but very functional shoes worn by the locals, but despite their seemingly affordable price, many children didn't have them. And not having shoes often meant they couldn't walk to school or travel to collect clean drinking water.

#**TEN**WORDS

BLAKE MYCOSKIE

Recognising the opportunity, Blake decided to do something about it. He started by buying just 250 pairs of alpargata's before he left Buenos Aires, pledging to make enough money from the sales to donate one pair for every pair sold. Over the next few years, Blake realised that selling high-margin items allowed him to build a retail model which was both commercially viable and socially aware, allowing him to give back significant proportions of his profits to the communities that made his products. For every pair of shoes sold, a pair is donated to a child from the area where they were produced. For each pair of glasses, an eye test is given. For each bag of TOMS coffee, clean water is provided. And for each bag sold, a birthing kit is donated to local midwives.

"I believe what we're doing is affecting the way businesses will be built for hundreds of years to come. Stay true to what you believe, and what your message is, and then let the chips fall where they fall."

So far, TOMS has donated over 70 million pairs of shoes to deprived children, helped to restore sight to 445,000 people, provided over 400,000 weeks of safe water and has supported safe birth services for 70,000 mothers. It is an incredible business model with incredible products. And what makes the model work so well is that marketing costs are at a minimum because feel-good purchases are shared at scale across social media and word-of-mouth generating the majority of new sales. As a result, 35% of sales come from social media alone. Impressive. What you stand for is indeed more important than what you sell.

#TENWORDS

SATYA NADELLA

"Our industry does not respect tradition – it only respects innovation".

"Always keep learning. If you don't you'll stop being useful". Ten words of advice worth remembering from Microsoft's CEO, Satya Nadella.

READ: Mindset by *Carl Dweck*
WATCH: Satya Nadella's Keynote at Dreamforce '15
FOLLOW: @SatyaNadella

Satya Nadella is a brave CEO. I'll never forget watching him give an unscripted keynote in front of 15,000 people at Dreamforce 2015, and then choosing to follow it with a live demo (from a Microsoft Surface and his iPhone) where everything could have gone wrong. Most CEO's would never even attempt this because the stakes (and chances of failure) are so high, but then again, Nadella is not your average CEO. It would have been easier for him to talk about the heritage and Microsoft and his vision for the future, but Nadella recognised that Microsoft needed more than a brand building exercise if it was to become more relevant and competitive.

"I have a one sentence philosophy for learning: Better to be a learn-it-all than a know-it-all".

Satya's philosophy is certainly working so far. In the few short years that he has been leading Microsoft, he has championed innovations such as voice control for the X-Box, developed HoloLens and Microsoft's virtual assistant Cortana as well improving their Azure "cloud services". There is a renewed sense of pride in the company which now boasts a culture not too dissimilar from Apple. Since he took over from Steve Ballmer as CEO in 2014, Nadella has re-invented Microsoft and increased their stock value by 60%. Not bad for a humble engineer who started out in the R&D department.

#**TEN**WORDS

"The journey of 1,000 miles begins with a single step."

LAU TZU

"Remember that even your worst days only have 24 hours."

ANON

"Time flies like an arrow. Fruit flies like a banana."

GROUCHO MARXTZU

"I will go anywhere as long as it is forward."

DAVID LIVINGSTON

"Try not. Do. Or do not. There is no try."

YODA

"I destroy my enemies when I make them my friends."

ABRAHAM LINCOLN

#TENWORDS

BARACK OBAMA

"Change only happens when ordinary people chose to get involved".

"One voice can change a room". President Barack Obama

READ: *Audacity of Hope* by Barack Obama
WATCH: President Obama's farewell address
FOLLOW: @BarackObama

Twenty months before Barack Obama was elected the 44th President of the United States, he needed to put together a team of staff to run his campaign. Despite the media hysteria surrounding his nomination, victory was by no means assured. Led by campaign manager David Plouffe (now SVP of Strategy at Uber), Obama recruited Facebook's head of PR Chris Hughes (Mark Zuckerberg's college roommate) to run his digital campaign. Unlike the campaigns of his rivals, John McCain or Hillary Clinton, Obama opted to break his manifesto promises down into media-friendly soundbites that the American public could understand – a strategy employed forty-eight years earlier by JFK when an Amercian's average attention span was believed to be around 42-seconds. By 2007 though, attention spans were hovering around 8-seconds so a different strategy was needed. Leading with a call to action of "*Change*" and a rallying cry of "*Yes we can*", Obama's campaign team communicated their messages using small words and short sentences. To connect with supporters faster and more efficiently, Chris Hughes created a fun-to-use social networking web site (MyBarackObama.com) that allowed Obama supporters to create groups, plan events, raise funds and download tools. By the time the campaign was over, volunteers had created more than 2 million profiles, planned 200,000 events, formed 35,000 groups, posted 400,000 blogs, and raised $30 million via 70,000 fund-raising pages.

#**TEN**WORDS

BARACK OBAMA

If there is one thing that seems to be evident in the eloquent language that most of the world's greatest storytellers use, it is the "rule of three". Eloquence is infectious. You notice a clever trick in the repertoire of a good speaker and you want to try it and use it yourself. One of the best pieces of advice I ever received was to study famous speeches, and see what makes them work. For superb orators like Obama, Churchill, Clinton and Mandela, they used the rule of three selectively to add impact to their speeches. To use it effectively, you peak on the third item. It is noted by speechwriters as being a triple with structural parallelism.

> *I was with you yesterday!*
> *I am with you today!*
> *And will be with you tomorrow!* [Loud applause].

Look at how Obama used it within his victory speech the evening that he won his campaign to become President.

> It's the **answer** told by lines that stretched around schools and churches – in numbers this nation has never seen....
> It's the *answer* spoken by young and old – rich and poor – Democrat and Republican...
> It's the *answer* that led those who've been told for so long, and by so many to be **cynical, and fearful, and doubtful**...
>
> It's been a long time coming – but tonight – because of what we did **on this day – in this election – at this defining moment** – change has come to America.

Next time you present, try it yourself. Pick three examples to re-enforce your point, and see what difference it makes – not just to your delivery, but to the reaction of your audience.

Obama's Rhetoric

The great speechwriter, Peggy Noonan (President Regan's speech writer and special assistant), once wrote, *"When big, serious, thoughtful things must be said, then, big serious, thoughtful speeches must be given."* I'll never forget when I watched President Barack Obama's farewell speech as he was about to end his final term as Commander-in-Chief when he gave a big, thoughtful speech about serious things. Big ideas, small words and short sentences. Here are a few of the things that I noticed which made the words of his speech so memorable:

The Rhetorical Devices

From the speech at the Democratic National Convention in 2004 that brought Obama to national prominence, to his final speech to the nation, Obama has mastered classic rhetorical devices that project power and confidence in communication. It's no coincidence that the following examples generated some of the biggest cheers of the night. 'Anaphora' is the repetition of the same word or words at the start of successive sentences or clauses. Obama is a master of this speech making technique.

"If I had told you eight years ago that America would reverse a great recession, reboot our auto industry, and unleash the longest stretch of job creation in our history... If I had told you that we would open up a new chapter with the Cuban people, shut down Iran's nuclear weapons program without firing a shot, take out the mastermind of 9-11... If I had told you that we would win marriage equality and secure the right to health insurance for another 20 million of our fellow citizens... If I had told you all that, you might have said our sights were set a little too high."

"Over the course of these eight years, I've seen the hopeful faces of young graduates and our newest military officers…I've seen our scientists help a paralyzed man regain his sense of touch. I've seen Wounded Warriors who at points were given up for dead, walk again. I've seen our doctors and volunteers rebuild after earthquakes and stop pandemics in their tracks. I've seen the youngest of children remind us through their actions and through their generosity of our obligations to care for refugees or work for peace."

"To all of you out there…Every organizer who moved to an unfamiliar town, every kind family who welcomed them in, every volunteer who knocked on doors, every young person who cast a ballot for the first time, every American who lived and breathed the hard work of change, you are the best supporters and organizers anybody could ever hope for, and I will forever be grateful. Because you did change the world."

Rule of Three

Obama uses the rule of three [called 'tricolons' in ancient Greek rhetoric] in paragraphs and within sentences themselves: *"grab a clip board, get some signatures, run for office."* Three is one of the most powerful numbers in communication. We think in threes, we group numbers in threes, we speak in threes, we remember words when they are clustered together in threes. Here are more examples from Obama's speech: *"We remain the wealthiest, the most powerful, the most respected nation on earth* [This is an example of 'ascending tricolon' which means the numbers of words increase in each part. It's very powerful]

"In just eight years we've halved our dependence on foreign oil, we've doubled our renewable energy, we've lead the world to an agreement that has the promise to save this planet."

"Yes. We. Can."

#TENWORDS

DAVID OGILVY

"One should use short words, short sentences and short paragraphs".

"The public is more interested in personalities than in corporations". David Ogilvy

On September 7th of 1982, advertising legend David Ogilvy sent an internal memo to all employees of his advertising agency, Ogilvy & Mather. The memo was entitled "*How to Write*" and contained the following list of advice. The better you write, the higher you go in Ogilvy & Mather. People who think well, write well. Woolly minded people write woolly memos, woolly letters and woolly speeches. Good writing is not a natural gift. You have to learn to write well.

10 Hints For Better Writing:
1. Read the Roman-Raphaelson book on writing. Read it three times.
2. Write the way you talk. Naturally.
3. Use short words, short sentences and short paragraphs.
4. Never use jargon words like reconceptualize, demassification, attitudinally, judgmentally. They are hallmarks of a pretentious ass.
5. Never write more than two pages on any subject.
6. Check your quotations.
7. Never send a letter or a memo on the day you write it. Read it aloud the next morning — and then edit it.
8. If it is something important, get a colleague to improve it.
9. Before you send your letter or your memo, make sure it is crystal clear what you want the recipient to do.
10. If you want ACTION, don't write. Go and tell the guy what you want.

READ: *Ogilvy on Advertising* by David Ogilvy
WATCH: Mad Men
FOLLOW: @Ogilvy

#TENWORDS

DAVID OGILVY

Lemon.

This Volkswagen missed the boat.

The chrome strip on the glove compartment is blemished and must be replaced. Chances are you wouldn't have noticed it; Inspector Kurt Kroner did.

There are 3,389 men at our Wolfsburg factory with only one job: to inspect Volkswagens at each stage of production. (3000 Volkswagens are produced daily; there are more inspectors than cars.)

Every shock absorber is tested (spot checking won't do), every windshield is scanned. VWs have been rejected for surface scratches barely visible to the eye.

Final inspection is really something! VW inspectors run each car off the line onto the Funktionsprüfstand (car test stand), tote up 189 check points, gun ahead to the automatic brake stand, and say "no" to one VW out of fifty.

This preoccupation with detail means the VW lasts longer and requires less maintenance, by and large, than other cars. (It also means a used VW depreciates less than any other car.)

We pluck the lemons; you get the plums.

Ogilvy's iconic "one-word" ad. Ogilvy was the king of the long form ad. He understood better than any other ad man the art of needing to get your attention in less than ten words, before asking you to read his copy.

#TENWORDS

JAMIE OLIVER

"I was in the right place at the right time".

Jamie is Britain's second best-selling author just behind J.K. Rowling. He says that his biggest challenge building his brand (via his books, TV shows and social media) is when he takes a simple idea, with a blank sheet of paper and then gets so excited creatively that he over-complicates the idea. His mission to simplify big ideas. He hasn't done too badly either, building a £160 million brand and creating over 8,000 jobs.

READ: Any one of his 22 books
WATCH: Jamie Oliver: Behind the Brand
FOLLOW: @JamieOliver

It's difficult to imagine that Jamie Oliver hasn't deliberately engineered his career as the world's most successful celebrity chef, but he has always seen himself as an accidental celebrity. It's one of the things that makes him most endearing to his audience, an audience which has helped him to build a brand of food evangelists who just want to encourage the world to eat better.

Jamie's big break came when he was asked to cover for someone who was off sick on the day that a film crew was coming in to record a documentary about the River Café where he worked. He was working in a particularly exciting part of the kitchen called "*Hots Two*" where the fritto misto, risottos and pasta were made. These were all really fast cooking dishes which would take a maximum of 90-seconds to make from beginning to end in a commercial kitchen. The dishes were very quick, they were very colourful, and the film crew soon realised that this was a TV makers dream. All the chefs in the kitchen were filmed that night, but when the program aired 6 months later, most of the documentary revolved around Jamie. Despite being very inexperienced, the twenty-year old Jamie was technically excellent in the kitchen. He came across on TV so well during those 90-second cameos that his phone started ringing with offers the very next day. Twenty-two years later he is still wowing audiences with big dishes for people with short attention spans.

#TEN WORDS

JIRO ONO

"Take your work seriously. Improve your skills. Focus on details".

After eating at Sukiyabashi Jiro, Barack Obama said it was *"the best sushi I've ever had in my life"*. French chef Joël Robuchon says that the restaurant is one of his favorites in the world, and taught him that sushi is an art.

READ: *Sushi* by Jiro Ono
WATCH: *Jiro Dreams of Sushi* by David Gelb
FOLLOW: Jiro's quest for excellence.

Sukiyabashi Jiro is a sushi restaurant in Ginza, Chūō, Tokyo, Japan owned and run by 91-year old Jiro Ono. It is the only restaurant of its kind, globally to be awarded three Michelin stars, the ultimate achievement for any restaurant. To put that in perspective, restaurants with three Michelin stars are held in such high regard, that people often travel to a country just to eat in one. Such an achievement conjures up images of silver service and grand dining rooms, but that is not what makes Sukiyabashi Jiro special. It is the food. And the way that the food is made. Nothing else. The restaurant itself is hidden away in a subway in Tokyo. It only has 10 seats, doesn't serve appetizers, most meals only last 15 minutes and it doesn't even have a bathroom inside the restaurant. But speak to any food critic or sushi master chef, and they will tell you it is one of the finest restaurants in the world.

Jiro loves to simplify complexity and exercises a great deal of self-discipline. He is a perfectionist who is never satisfied with his work, wanting every next dish to be better than the last, and it's all he seems to think about from the moment he gets up to the moment he falls asleep. Ask Jiro's friends about what motivates him and they will talk about his strong leadership and infectious passion, but ask Jiro about the real secret to his success and he will mention just ten words: "Take your work seriously. Improve your skills. Focus on details"

#**TEN**WORDS

GEORGE ORWELL

"Enlightened people seldom or never possess a sense of responsibility".

George Orwell is one of the best satirists of modern times. Through his books, articles and essays, he challenged people to think differently, often by saying one thing when he meant the opposite. This quote is a perfect example because Orwell felt a great responsibility to write and I'm pretty sure he considered himself *"enlightened"*. In his essay *Why I Write*, he explained that his compulsion to write came from a desire to expose lies or facts *"to which I want to draw attention"*. He felt a deep responsibility to share any injustices that he saw with his audience. Of course, Orwell's ten words appear to imply the exact opposite, but he understood the need to lead with satire or a provocative statement in order to get people's attention. When Orwell was once asked why he felt *so* compelled to share his opinions, he replied beautifully: *"In a time of universal deceit – telling the truth is a revolutionary act"*. A statement as true today as it was over 70 years ago.

During his tragically short life, George Orwell (1903-1950) wrote nine books but is most famously known for writing the original 'Big Brother' story *"1984"* and the political satire *"Animal Farm"*. Orwell's work continues to influence popular and political culture today through the terms he coined such as Cold War, Big Brother, Thought Police, Room 101, Memory Hole, Newspeak, Doublethink, and Thought-crime.

READ: *Why I Write* by George Orwell
WATCH: *1984*: The screenplay by Michael Radford
FOLLOW: @OrwellQuotes | @TheOrwellPrize

Orwell's Six Rules for Writers
1. Never use a figure of speech which you are used to seeing.
2. Never use a long word where a short word will do.
3. If it is possible to cut a word out, always cut it out.
4. Never use the passive where you can use the active.
5. Never use jargon or a scientific word if you can think of an everyday equivalent.
6. Break any of these rules sooner than say anything outright barbarous.

#TENWORDS

JOEL OSTEEN

"You can change your whole world by changing your words".

Each week, Joel Osteen delivers a sermon to an audience of over 7 million. Joel got over his fear of public speaking by writing every 28-minute message word-for-word and then practicing it all day Thursday and Friday. It took him 18-months of being scared of speaking every week before he finally realised *"I was meant to do this"*.

READ: *Your Best Life Now* by Joel Osteen
WATCH: *Words of Art* by Jeff Roldan
FOLLOW: @JoelOsteen

On June 7, 2014, I watched Houston-based Pastor Joel Osteen take the stage at a sold-out Yankee Stadium to deliver a sermon in front of 50,000 people. Many of those in attendance that Saturday night were no doubt part of Osteen's global television audience, which now extends to viewers in more than 100 countries. The Yankee Stadium appearance was unthinkable just 15 years earlier because Osteen himself never dreamed it would be possible.

"Life is 10% what happens to you and 90% how you respond".

Osteen took over as pastor of Lakewood Church after his father passed away. John Osteen had started Lakewood in an abandoned Houston feed store and had grown the church to about 6,000 members when his son took over. Joel had no intention of preaching. For seventeen years he was perfectly content behind the scenes, producing his father's television broadcast. In fact, he *"dreaded"* public speaking. Joel had only ever preached once in his life—the week before his dad unexpectedly passed away. And he was a nervous wreck. Joel Osteen's journey to become the face of the largest church in America and one of the most influential Christian leaders in the world is an inspiring story of personal transformation. He now leads a congregation of over 45,000 people and is recognised as one of the world's best speakers.

#TENWORDS

General GEORGE S. PATTON

"Holding our position? We are not holding a Goddamned thing".

"A good plan violently executed now, is better than a perfect plan executed next week". General George S. Patton.

When George Smith Patton spoke, people listened. He was a highly controversial general of the U.S. Army best known for his leadership of the U.S. Army during World War II and being instrumental in liberating Germany from the Nazis. Patton is considered one of the most successful combat generals in U.S. history, but at the time, his colourful words and controversial statements alienated people. Patton didn't care. The only audience he wanted to inspire were the men under his command. And that he did. So when Patton spoke these ten words to his troops before D-Day during World War II in 1945, his men were left in no doubt that they needed to advance forward. But this was no blind rallying cry. Patton had built his career on earning the trust of his men by taking *"calculated risks"* which won battles and saved lives.

Patton was a wartime leader. And wartime leaders speak differently from peacetime leaders. Leaders who lead during challenging times need to choose their words carefully. The wrong sentences at the wrong times don't just cause bad PR, they cause people to die. So when Patton was questioned about his direct approach (in an era when few public figures swore) he replied, *"When I want my men to remember something important, to really make it stick, I give it to them double dirty. You can't run an army without profanity, and it was to be* **eloquent profanity**".

READ: *War as I Knew It* by Goerge S. Patton
WATCH: *Patton* by Franklin J. Schaffner
FOLLOW: His advice.

#TENWORDS

TOM PETERS

"Hustle. Be prepared. Keep some clever research up your sleeve".

Tom Peters *(ex-McKinsey & Co)* is regarded as one of the world's finest management consultants. At every opportunity, he reminds executives of the four most important words in business: *"What. Do. You. Think?"*

READ: *Re-Imagine!* By Tom Peters
WATCH: "3 Ways to Pursue Excellence"
FOLLOW: @Tom_Peters

Tom Peters is one of the world's most successful management consultants, who is famous for charging up to $50K per hour for his time. Of course that figure sounds like a disgustingly large amount but it is all relative. One hour of consulting with Tom could (and has) saved organisations millions of dollars from making bad decisions. Tom has worked really hard to get to where he has got to in the cut throat world of management consulting, but it's fair to say he knows his stuff.

So when I once asked him for the best piece of advice he could give to someone like me, someone about to embark upon a career in the corporate world, he shared with me these ten words. I'm paraphrasing, but he told me that there were only ever three things I needed to do in order to be successful in a large organisation.

1. Work harder than everyone else.
2. Go into every meeting more prepared than everyone else.
3. Always have a clever piece of research up your sleeve.

The first is obvious. The second is common sense and yet still very few people prepare properly. The third helps you to add value to any meeting and wins you the respect of colleagues or customers, regardless of your job title, level of experience or salary. $50,000 of advice. Done.

#**TEN**WORDS

MIUCCIA PRADA

"It's horrible when people are only interested in buying labels".

When Miuccia Prada took over the family luxury goods business in 1978 it was making around $480,000 per year. Today the Prada brand is worth $9.5 Billion making Miuccia (according to Forbes) the 75th most powerful woman in the world.

READ: *Prada* by Patrizio and Michael Rock
WATCH: Any interviews with Miuccia Prada
FOLLOW: @Prada

Ten years ago I wrote a book called "Sex, Brands and Rock'n'Roll". It was more of a manifesto for my agency than a book, and it opened with a quote I heard Miuccia Prada give in a Vogue interview at the time, *"Buying a $5,000 handbag as a status symbol is a sign of weakness"*. It was a quote which stuck with me because, at the time, I was attending a church in the North of England run by a brilliant pastor called Paul Scanlon. I'll never forget the day he gave a sermon and told a story about his £500 Prada boots. He was talking about how we should *"love our neighbours as ourselves"*, and therefore if we had the means, we should love ourselves with Prada shoes and not feel guilty about it. His contention was that if you loved yourself that much, you might love your neighbours even more. His words received a very mixed reaction from the audience. I admire the sentiment, but I'm still not convinced by the message.

Miuccia Prada challenges me in a similar way. Despite the fact that she sells expensive designer labels, she argues that *"It's horrible when people are only interested in buying labels. Because it doesn't bring them the happiness that they think it will"*. Buying £500 shoes or a $5,000 handbag is not a bad thing. Just like money is not the root of all evil. But the *"love of money"* or having the desire for a designer label to turn you into something that impresses other people, *that's* where the problems start.

#TENWORDS

TONY ROBBINS

"What's your motivation? What's great? What's missing? What's preventing this?"

Tony Robbins is a big man with a huge heart and an even bigger personality. His personality and leadership style is so extreme that people either love him or hate him. I'm a big fan. And so, it seems, are the 200,000 people that he presents to in 12 countries EVERY year.

[Presenting advice] *"You shouldn't practice until you get it right, you should practice until you never get it wrong".*

READ: *Money Matters* by Tony Robbins
WATCH: *I Am Not Your Guru* on Netflix
FOLLOW: @TonyRobbins

Tony Robbins is the best speaker I have ever seen in real-life (and I've seen some impressive speakers in my time). I'll never forget the first time I saw him. I was invited as a guest and was seated very close to the front row. I was in the Moscone Center in San Francisco with 20,000 other people, and millions more watching the livestream. Tony spoke for almost four hours, with only a couple of slides and a few pieces of paper as notes. His whole presentation focused on the ten words above, and it was one of the best presentations I have ever seen. Time flew past so quickly it felt more like a TED talk than a four-hour seminar. People were jumping in the aisles. Others were crying. Even the most conservative chief executives were losing their inhibitions and roleplaying with strangers. It was quite a sight to behold. Robbins said many things over those four hours, but there is one quote I have never forgotten. *"You need to ask 'Why' seven times before you discover the real problem because the problem you think you are facing is usually never the problem"*.

I saw the truth of this first hand when the Japanese CEO of a large automotive brand said his biggest challenge was *"staying innovative"*. Tony nodded but wasn't convinced. Seven *"whys"* and a few direct questions later, the exec tearfully admitted that his employees didn't trust him. It was in that moment that I truly understood the power of asking, **"Why?"**.

#TENWORDS

KEVIN ROBERTS

"Brands must create 'Loyalty Beyond Reason' in order to survive".

As the CEO of Saatchi & Saatchi, Kevin Roberts turned the world's largest ad agency into an *"Ideas Factory"*, encouraging the 7,000 creatives under his command to create *"loyalty beyond reason"* for the brands that they represented (including P&G, Lexus, Toyota, Mini, Tiffany's and the BBC).

READ: Lovemarks by Kevin Roberts
WATCH: It's the Idea, Not the Technology (YouTube)
FOLLOW: @KRconnect

Alongside *Purple Cow (*Seth Godin*)* and *How to Win Friends (*Dale Carnegie*), Lovemarks* by Kevin Roberts is one of the top three business books I have ever read. Written the year after Facebook was founded in 2005, it talks about how consumers make decisions with their hearts and justify them with their heads. He talks about what makes truly *great* advertising, something he knew a little bit about as the CEO of Saatchi and Saatchi.

Kevin introduced me to the concept of *"loyalty beyond reason"* when he spoke to me about an April fools stunt to stop making Heinz Tomato ketchup. Consumers of the red sauce were so distraught that one of their most favourite brands was being discontinued that they formed forums, community groups, and media teams in order to campaign for its reinstatement. Of course, it was all a publicity stunt but it showed the level of loyalty than many fans have for that iconic brand. Brands such as Heinz, Nike, Apple and Harley-Davidson have it. Others do not. Kevin calls the brands that do, *"Lovemarks"*. If you discontinued a product and thousands of people are not setting up Facebook fan pages to save it, chances are your brand is not a *lovemark*. Despite being 12 years old, I encourage you to read this brilliant book. Because despite the speed that the world is changing, one thing that will never change is the fact that we will always make decisions with our hearts and justify them with our heads.

#**TEN**WORDS

KEVIN ROBERTS

Brand	Lovemark
Information	Relationship
Recognised by Customers	Loved by People
Generic	Personal
Presents a Narrative	Creates a Love Story
The Promise of Quality	The Touch of Sensuality
Symbolic	Iconic
Defined	Infused
Statement	Story
Defined Attributes	Wrapped in Mystery
Values	Spirit
Professional	Passionately Creative
Advertising Agency	Ideas Company

#TENWORDS

GINNI ROMETTY

"Your value isn't what you know, it's what you share".

When I first heard Ginni's ten words of advice to the 380,000 IBMers under her leadership, it reminded me of a statement I heard from the CEO of Linkedin, *"The value of your services is greater than the value of the services you provide"*. Both statements, from leaders in charge of two tech giants, struck a chord with me as the one thing that many people working in large organisations miss: Knowing things is worthless unless you share them. If there is one thing Ginni is brilliant at, it is sharing complicated information with people in a language that all of them can understand. Despite being an engineer by trade, she doesn't over-complicate her messages – whether she is sharing her vision of the future with shareholders or discussing the nuances between *"augmented"* and *"artificial"* intelligence with primary school children, simplifying complex messages is one of the things I admire most about Ginni.

I was already impressed after hearing Ginni speak at CES in 2016 about IBM's vision of *"the cognitive era"*, but when I discovered that IBM's super-computer *"Watson"* was helping doctors to save the lives of premature babies, I knew I had to join the company. Having identical twin daughters of my own (both premature and surviving against all the odds), I wanted to work for a company that was making a difference. Watson, like Ginni, understands that sharing information is far more powerful than just knowing it.

Under Ginni's leadership as CEO, chairman and president, IBM has registered more patents than any other company in the world for the 24th consecutive running. Ranked the 6th most valuable brand in the world according to Interbrand, IBM has the world's largest industrial research department which is home to 5 Nobel prize winners.

READ: Intro to IBM's 2016 Annual Report (*Seriously*).
WATCH: Ginni speaking @WEF #Davos2017
FOLLOW: @IBM | @IBMWatson

#TENWORDS

J.K. ROWLING

"The stories we love best do live in us forever.".

"You have to resign yourself to wasting lots of trees before you write anything really good".

J.K. Rowling has sold over 450 million books. In 2004, Forbes declared her the first person to become a billionaire primarily through book writing. Today, the Harry Potter franchise is valued at $24 Billion.

READ: *The Casual Vacancy* by J.K. Rowling
WATCH: Rowling's Harvard Commencement Speech
FOLLOW: @JK_Rowling

J.K. Rowling wrote her initial Potter ideas on a napkin whilst on a delayed train from Manchester to London in 1990. She was always good at improvising when she had a story inside her bursting to get out, and could never wait to get home and be surrounded by the perfect writing conditions. When she is hit by inspiration, she has to write immediately because she doesn't want to see a good story *"escape"*. I love that sense of urgency. It is why I carry a notebook with me everywhere I go.

"I can write anywhere. I made up the names of the characters [for Harry Potter] on a sick bag while I was on an airplane."

J.K. Rowling famously typed her first book, *Harry Potter and the Philosopher's Stone* on a manual typewriter, after writing the story in *The Elephant House Coffee Shop* by Edinburgh Castle. She would go there, with her limited welfare money, and wait until her baby daughter Jessica was asleep, and then order an espresso and a glass of water before writing for as long as she could. Despite her literary brilliance and poverty-fueled creativity, twelve publishing houses rejected the original Harry Potter 'coffee shop' manuscripts. Eventually, a small London based publisher called Bloomsbury gave her a chance with an advance of £1,500 and a modest print run of 1,000 copies. Little did they know it would become the best-selling book series in history.

#TENWORDS

BABE RUTH

"Every strike brings me closer to the next home run".

George Herman "Babe" Ruth Jr. won 89 games in six seasons with the Boston Red Sox, including 24 in 1917, and helped the team win three World Series titles. He changed the game of baseball with his ten word philosophy, *"You just can't beat the person who never gives up".*

READ: *Babe: The Legend* by Robert Creamer
WATCH: The Babe with John Goodman
FOLLOW: @RedSox

On the afternoon of July 11, 1914, a husky 19-year-old starting pitcher for the Boston Red Sox called George Herman Ruth Jr made his major-league baseball debut by earning a victory against the visiting Cleveland Naps. None of the 11,087 fans in attendance at Fenway Park could have known that Boston's rookie southpaw, who was hitless in the game, would change the game and become a baseball legend, still recognised a century later by just his nickname the *"Babe."* Over the course of his career, Ruth went on to break baseball's most important records, including years leading a league in home runs (12), most bases in a season (457) and highest slugging percentage (.847). Although best remembered by baseball fans for swatting a prodigious 714 home runs and slugging .690, which remains a major-league record, I remember Babe Ruth fondly because of his failures. His ten word mantra *"Every strike brings me closer to the next home run"* is not a statement of success, it is a statement of failure. Despite being the greatest baseball player ever to swing a bat, his batting average was .342. That means for every 1,000 pitches he missed 648 of them. In baseball a success rate of one in three gets you into the hall of fame. So why is it that we struggle so much with failure in business? If only 34% of my presentations were successful I'd be devastated. But what if I changed my attitude to think that every failed presentation just brings me one step closer to success?

#**TEN**WORDS

SHERYL SANDBERG

"Employ people who can take feedback, because they learn quickly".

As Facebook's COO, Sheryl Sandberg is arguably the most influential woman in business. Sheryl is the author of the bestselling book "*Lean In: Women, Work, and the Will to Lead*" which explores why women's voices are not always heard in the workplace. It has sold over 1 million copies.

READ: Sheryl Sandberg's "*Option B*" Facebook Post
WATCH: Sheryl's "*Women Leaders*" TED Talk
FOLLOW: Sheryl on Facebook (*obviously*).

The one thing that seems to unite the best tech executives is their obsession with speed. Benioff says companies are competing against speed. Zuckerberg wants to move fast and break things. Ginni Rometty talks about survival of the fastest. Bill Gates employs lazy people to solve problems because he thinks they'll find a solution fastest. Sheryl Sandberg wants people to *learn* faster, *lead* faster and *share stories* faster.

"*If you please everyone, you are not making enough progress*".

"*Fast growth means you are always behind,*" says Facebook COO Sheryl Sandberg. It's a nice problem to have and one that she faced in 2008 when she quit her secure job at Google as VP of operations to join Facebook as the No. 2 to the then-23-year-old CEO and founder Mark Zuckerberg. Facebook had just 550 employees at the time. Sheryl had built her business unit at Google from four to 4,000 people in five years and understood how to "*scale*" a business. It is her business savvy that has helped Zuckerberg to employ over 17,000 people at Facebook today. "*You can never hire the right people too early and you often hire them too late.*" Legend has it that Sheryl landed her job at Facebook, not because of her impressive CV, but because her opening line was just one sentence: "*Tell me what your biggest problem is and I'll find a way to fix it*".

#TENWORDS

CHARLES SCHULTZ

"There's a difference between a philosophy and a bumper sticker".

"Happiness is a warm puppy!"

Between 1950 and 2000 Charles Schultz wrote 17,897 comic strips. Beginning as a hobby alongside his day job, Peanuts developed into the world's most popular cartoon strip, syndicated for 2,600 newspapers in 75 countries and 25 languages.

READ: *Peanuts* by Charles Schultz
WATCH: *Charles Schultz* : A Documentary
FOLLOW: @Snoopy

Charles Schultz knows a thing or two about bumper stickers since there are more Peanut's inspired bumper stickers than any other cartoon character in the world. He also knew a few things about philosophy from working as a typesetter in a Roman Catholic youth magazine where he also wrote religious cartoons. Charles wrote slogans that he hoped would make people smile, such as *"I have a new philosophy. I'm going to dread one day at a time"* and *"I think I've discovered the secret of life – you just hang around until you get used to it"*. As a cartoonist, he built his career upon one sentence stories and bumper sticker quotes, but his words always had a deeper meaning. All Charles ever wanted to do was inspire people through his art without preaching.

"The way I see it, it doesn't matter what you believe just so you're sincere".

Charles did a great job. Not only did he build a multi-million dollar franchise, but through his short stories, he brightened people's day. Every time Charlie Brown missed kicking the football, he was indirectly encouraging his readers to never give up. Linus's blanket was a metaphor for the security blankets we all need from time to time. Lucy knew her worth as a girl, charging 5 cents for advice and every Peanuts strip was reminding us not to take life too seriously. According to Charles, the fastest way to make a difference - is to make people smile.

#**TEN**WORDS

CHARLES SCHULTZ

I'd say I'm about
one cookie away
from being happy.

#TENWORDS

JERRY SEINFELD

"The road less travelled is less travelled for a reason".

Jerry Seinfeld doesn't like people very much. I've heard him admit it many times, and he's not just trying to be funny. He really doesn't. That's why he loves the simplicity of stand-up more than working with the complex teams required to make a TV show. This may seem odd coming from a man whose TV show made him the world's highest paid comedian, but it is the raw energy of being in front of a live audience which drives him. *"No one is more judged in civilized society than a standup comedian. Every 12 seconds you're rated."*

Jerry's success is rooted in the fact that he cares more about what his audience thinks, than what he thinks. *"I'm not that big on enjoyment. I don't think it's that important. I think what's important is that they enjoy it"*. So, to make sure *that they do "enjoy it",* he reminds himself of three questions before each gig:

1. Will my audience like my material?
2. How do I live up to expectations after a good performance?
3. How do I make sure my stories stick?

Being a standup comedian is hard. The nights that you bomb in front of a live audience can be brutal and soul destroying. You need quick wits, fast communication skills *and* a thick skin to cope with instant *"feedback"* and rejection. This is why they are not many *great* comedians who last. *"The road less travelled is less travelled for a reason".*

Jerry Seinfeld is the most commercially successful comedian of all-time. He was also the co-creator and co-writer of *Seinfeld*, the long-running sitcom which has received numerous awards and was claimed to have the "Top TV Episode of All-Time". At the peak of the show, Seinfeld was making $267 million (1998). Almost 20 years later he is still making over $30 million a year.

READ: *The Seinfeld Scripts*
WATCH: *Comedians in Cars Getting Coffee*
FOLLOW: @JerrySeinfeld

"People think the comedian leads the audience. He doesn't really. He rides a wave that can crush you at any time. While you're doing your maneuvers you look like you're in control, but you're really not."

JERRY SEINFELD

#TENWORDS

RICCARDO SEMLER

"The key to management is to get rid of managers".

"If you are giving back, you took too much."

Ricardo Semler is the CEO and majority owner of Semco Partners, a Brazilian company best known for its radical form of industrial democracy and corporate re-engineering. He prefers to share his profits immediately with his employees, rather than keep the money and give it back later.

READ: *Maverick* by Ricardo Semler
WATCH: Ricardo's *"No Rules"* TED Talk (2014)
FOLLOW: His leadership advice. All of it.

Whenever I hear the famous Peter Drucker quote *"Culture eats strategy for breakfast"*, I immediately think of Ricardo Semler. It takes a brave CEO to flatten any corporate hierarchy, but that's exactly what Ricardo did. He was convinced that in order for his business to grow, he needed his employees to trust him and he needed to reduce the number of managers who were making rules that governed their holidays, promotions and working hours. He believed that managers were often untrusted by employees, so he took them away and let individuals and teams govern themselves. The results were remarkable.

"For a company to excel, employees must be reassured that self-interest, not the company's, is their foremost priority. We believe an employee who puts himself first will be motivated to perform."

Over the course of a decade, Ricardo grew his modest construction company in Brazil from a $4M business to a billion dollar organisation, largely as a result of the way that he restructured the company by removing management structures.

"The purpose of work is not to make money. The purpose of work is to make workers, feel good about life."

Watch his TED talk and read his book. I promise, you won't be disappointed.

#TENWORDS

JASON SILVA

"I make videos that are like philosophical shots of espresso".

Jason Silva is a media artist, futurist and philosopher. He is the creator of Shots of Awe, a short film series of "*trailers for the mind*" that serve as *"philosophical espresso shots"* about technology creativity, futurism and metaphysics. He is also the Emmy nominated host of National Geographic Channel's hit TV series, Brain Games, airing in over 100 countries.

READ: *Existentialism & Humanism* by J.P. Satre
WATCH: *Shots of Awe*
FOLLOW: @Jason Silva

The first time I used a video during one of my keynotes which received an audible gasp from the audience was when I showed one of Jason's *"philosophical espresso shots"*. These 90 second videos consist of Jason telling a story about a particular technology whilst talking twice as fast as any human should be allowed. The videos worked really well in the UK and US, but when I started to spend more time in Europe, the audience struggled because of the speed of his words. (I learned the script myself and delivered it at a slower pace). Jason is one of those incredible people whose mind operates even faster than his mouth. He started creating "*shots of awe*" videos back in 2013 just for fun. They now boast over 13 million views and have been picked up by Discovery Networks.

Many people in this book favour short sentences and small words but Jason doesn't reduce the size of his sentences or his words, he just increases the speed of them. But this isn't quantity at the expense of quality. As someone who studies neuroscience, Jason is so obsessive about attention spans that his videos are scientifically edited to keep your attention from beginning until to end. It's almost impossible to multitask if you're watching one of his "shots" because he crams so much information into them. I love them, but I still find myself needing to take a breath and a moment of silence to process all the information once I've watched one.

#TENWORDS

NATE SILVER

"We need to admit that we have a prediction problem".

What makes him successful is the way that he analyses information. He is not just hunting for patterns. So when Jon Stewart interviewed statistician Nate Silver on the Daily Show, he called him *"The God of the Algorithm"*. Nate claimed he was just an Excel ninja trying to challenge himself and others.

READ: *The Signal and the Noise* by Nate Silver
WATCH: *The Art and Science of Prediction*
FOLLOW: @NateSilver538

Nobody does predictions better than Nate Silver. In the 2008 US presidential election, Nate Silver correctly predicted the winner of 49 of the 50 states. He also predicted the winner of all 35 U.S. Senate races that year and all 50 states (including the District of Columbia) in the 2012 presidential election. He got 2016 wrong. Why? Because Nate he acted more like a pundit and less like an unbiased analyst when he called Hillary to win the election over Trump.

"Before we demand more of our data, we need to demand more of ourselves".

Nate isn't on his own. Various marketing research papers I have read suggest that two-thirds of organisations now have no idea what their customers are going to do next. And these were companies who felt that they previously understood their customers very well. What statisticians never fully understand is the context behind the data, and that people lie, which often makes the data obsolete. They say publicly they will vote one way, then they vote differently in private. Whilst statistics can be classed as *"the science of finding relationships and actionable insights from data"* science is often based upon a lot of assumptions. Nate's advice? *"We must become more comfortable with probability and uncertainty."* Understanding data is important. But the challenge for all of us is to understand the stories behind the data.

#TENWORDS

RAF SIMONS

"You must make sure there are sublime moments everyday".

"The fashion world doesn't know when to stop, so you have to make sure there are sublime moments everyday". Raf Simons

It's sometimes difficult to get excited about the future. It's much easier for most of us to look back on the past with a warm sense of nostalgia. Raf Simons is not one of those people. I was introduced to him when I first saw Dior & I, now one of my favourite documentaries. The story follows Raf Simons (ex-creative director of Jill Sander) as the newly appointed creative director of Christian Dior, tasked with modernising one of the world's most iconic and traditional brands. He has some new and extreme ideas for taking Dior forward, but his challenge is respecting the history of the brand and the legacy of the past.

"The future for me is romantic. I don't understand people who say the past is romantic. Romantic for me is something you don't know yet. Something you can dream about. Something unknown and mystical..."

Raf succeeds by balancing the original and the modern perfectly, but only because he sees the future differently to everyone else. The ateliers and management at Dior were very precious about the past and were resistant to change, but they realised that the *"maison"* needed to move forward. Clinging to his ten word philosophy, Raf remained positive, despite the challenges and corporate politics that he encountered. It's a beautiful film for anyone working with established brands who are wishing to *"transform"* themselves.

READ: *Dior on Dior* by Christian Dior
WATCH: *Dior & I* by Frédéric Tcheng
FOLLOW: @CalvinKlein *(Raf is now Creative Director)*

#TENWORDS

SIMON SINEK

"I want to inspire others to do what inspires them".

Sinek is one of my favourite humans. He has inspired millions of people with his *"golden circle"* explanation of *What*, *How* and *Why*? From his book *Start With Why*. His TED talk is now one of the most watched presentations of all-time.

READ: *Start With Why* by Simon Sinek
WATCH: Any of his keynotes on YouTube.
FOLLOW: @SimonSinek

Simon Sinek is one of my favourite speakers. His wildly successful TEDx talk *"How great leaders inspire action"* came from his book Start With Why. When I first heard it back in 2011 it knocked my socks off. I have watched it countless times since then and have shared it with thousands of people during my own keynotes. It still inspires me every time that I watch it. Despite Sinek's three thousand word presentation lasting just a few seconds over eighteen minutes, his short flip chart session managed to change the way that millions of people think about their businesses and their careers. Changing the world (or your industry) doesn't always need to involve a huge event or a significant act, it could be just a few carefully chosen words, to the right audience, at the right time.

At the core of Simon's talk was the idea that *"People don't buy what you do they buy why you do it"* because *"the goal is not to do business with everybody who needs what you have. The goal is to do business with people who believe what you believe"*. Sinek has dedicated his career to helping people find their *"why"* – that one thing that gives purpose to whatever they do. When asked a few years later what his own why was he simply said, *"I want to inspire others to do what inspires them"*. It may have taken Sinek 3,006 words to make his mark on the world, but it only took ten words to explain *why* he did it.

#**TEN**WORDS

SIMON SINEK

"There is a difference between offering a service and being willing to serve.

They both include giving, but only one is generous„."

Sometimes you hear such a beautiful quote that you need to write it down immediately. I scribbled this down the second I heard Simon say it because I was worried I'd forget it. For Sinek, this was his 'next ten words' (to use the political debating phrase and not literally the word count) describing how his "why" was to inspire people to serve.

The Golden Circle
By @SimonSinek

The golden circle is based upon a very simple premise. Many people know what they do, some know how they do it, but very few people ever stop to examine exactly why they do it. Brands *"sell"* in the same way. They tell their customers what they do and how they do it, but they often fail to communicate why they do it. They think from the outside in. The most successful brands, on the other hand, think from the inside out. They tell people why their company exists, and then they go on to explain how they do it and lastly what they sell. The most successful companies think from the inside out ~ but in order to do that, they must first know their purpose and be able to communicate it well.

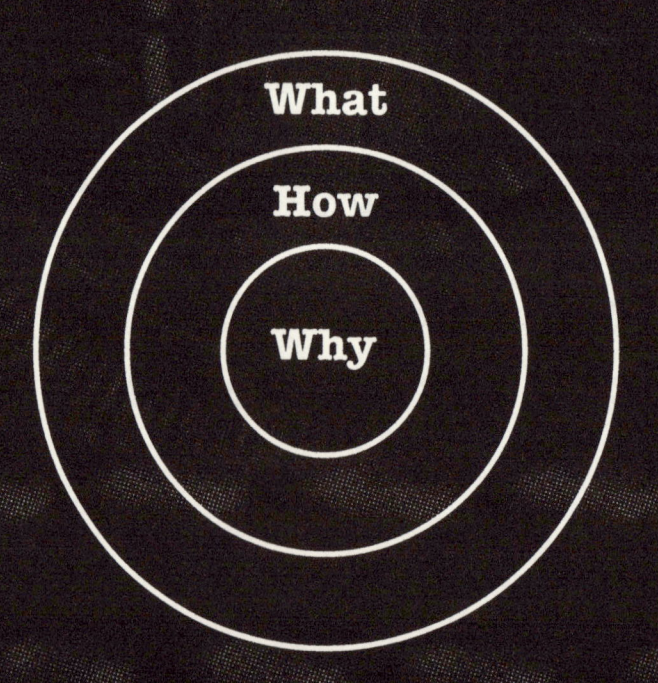

What

How

Why

#TENWORDS

WILL SMITH

"You need to understand exactly what makes a commercial success".

"Too many people spend money they haven't earned, to buy things they don't want, to impress people they don't like".

READ: Pursuit of Happyness by Chris Gardner
WATCH: Will Smith at IBM Amplify 2017
LISTEN: The Fresh Prince & DJ Jazzy Jeff

Will Smith always wanted to be one of the biggest movie stars in the world. Some movie stars accidentally stumble upon stardom or as a result of a breakthrough movie but Will Smith didn't have either, nor did he like Hollywood's odds of success. He decided instead to engineer his career much like a content marketer would. He shared his story at IBM's Amplify marketing conference in early 2017, where he said that any ambitious professional, in any profession, needs to *"begin with the end in mind"*. During his interview, Will explained exactly how he planned on becoming the world's biggest movie star. *"Storytelling is everything"*, he told the Amplify audience, before he dropped his killer ten words: *"You need to understand exactly what makes a commercial success"*. So, Will studied the most successful box office hits of all time and made three simple observations.

1. The top 10 grossing movies of all-time were special effects films.
2. 9/10 involved a creature of some kind.
3. 8/10 involved a love story.

Will then decided to only star in films which were most likely to become box office hits because they ticked these three boxes (*Independence Day, iRobot, Men in Black, I am Legend*). This approach made him one of Hollywood's biggest stars and has allowed him to focus on the smaller projects he really believes in like *The Pursuit of Happyness*.

#TENWORDS

Sir PAUL SMITH

"Balance your dreams and the reality of what you do".

"Experience is the best teacher. A compelling story is a close second".

Since 1970 Sir Paul Smith has built a fashion brand that makes *"classic clothes with a twist"*. He has been knighted, makes over $200 million a year and is one of the most humble business person you'll ever meet.

VISIT: Paul Smith's flagship store in Covent Garden
WATCH: Paul Smith: Gentleman Designer
FOLLOW: @PaulSmithDesign on Instagram

Many designers who have been around a while, especially if they are fortunate enough to have been knighted by The Queen, may be forgiven for relying on their legacy. It's a bit like Mick Jagger being brilliant, but choosing to spend decades rolling out the same hits to an adoring audience that knows exactly what to expect. Paul Smith doesn't like rolling out the same hits. No, like some other artists and designers in this book, Paul Smith takes a 'hands-on' approach to the creative process seeing himself as a *"commercial artist"*. Sir Paul Smith, now 70, is as excited about designing for the next season as he was when he started out from his modest Nottingham shop in 1970. It was a shop no bigger than the average person's spare bedroom (12 square feet) and it didn't even have any windows.

"Fashion is about today and tomorrow. Nobody cares how good you used to be".

Paul is officially the nicest man in fashion and often wanders around his stores talking to customers. He is regularly seen chatting for ages to tourists and fashion bloggers. He just loves people. And he loves listening to what they like. His success is founded on hard graft, honesty, a twinkly-eyed eternal optimism and good manners. Sir Paul shows that you don't *have* to be a self-serving megalomaniac to be successful in business.

#TENWORDS

PATTI SMITH

"Oh, to be reborn within the pages of a book".

"I would rather write or record something great and have it overlooked than do mediocre work and have it be popular". Patti Smith

READ: *Patti Smith: Complete* by Patti Smith
WATCH: *Patti Smith: Dream of a Life*
LISTEN: *Horses* by Patti Smith

I wasn't old enough to appreciate Patti Smith at the height of her popularity, but when I was doing an event early on in my career in Manchester and I heard Tim Booth, the lead single of James (one of my favourite bands), dedicating his career to her, I was desperate to understand what made her so special. So powerful was the impact that Patti Smith's lyrics had on a young Tim Booth that he said, "I went out and bought 'Horses' the next day. The next week I put up a sign selling everything I had. I decided that I would not have anything if it was not as strong as Horses". Strong words. Words which drove Tim to become the singer/songwriter for one of the most successful bands of the 1990's.

Patti is known mainly as a singer songwriter, but she is also a visionary punk poet, an artist, and such an accomplished photographer that some of her work features in MoMA in New York. Morrissey said she inspired him to form The Smiths and Michael Stipe credits her as being the reason he formed R.E.M. Not too bad for a self-conscious skinny girl who couldn't afford art college so she trained as a teacher instead. So inspired was she by Andy Warhol's first ever retrospective show, that she escaped to New York in 1967, with only $16 in her pocket, desperate to follow her dreams. She had no plan B. This book is full of people who are famous for ten words, but as with Patti and Tim, it is what happens *after* you hear those words that makes *all* the difference.

#TENWORDS

AARON SORKIN

"The story doesn't really begin until you've introduced the intention".

Aaron Sorkin is the Emmy award winning writer of The West Wing but he secured his place in history when he won an Academy Award and a BATFA in 2011 for 'Best Adapted Screenplay' for *The Social Network*. You may be familiar his movies but you should check out his massively underrated *News Room* and *Studio 60*. You won't be disappointed.

READ: Masterclass.com with Aaron Sorkin
WATCH: The West Wing
FOLLOW: The West Wing Weekly podcast

If it wasn't for Aaron Sorkin, *"Ten Words"* would not exist. He is responsible for igniting my love of writing, for helping me to understand the structure of a presentation and for the title of this book. *"Ten Words"* was taken from an episode of The West Wing called *Game On* where the characters in the White House are trying to find a ten word statement that helps them win the presidential debate, by summarising their manifesto in one short statement. (The full explanation is at the beginning of this book in case you missed it).

Aaron graduated from Syracuse University in Musical Theatre, but it was a serious piece of writing which got him his big break. Working as a bar tender in New York in order to pay his rent, Sorkin wrote a script about the U.S. Navy on cocktail napkins in between shifts. The play became '*A Few Good Men*' and it received such good reviews from the stage, that it was turned into the blockbuster movie featuring Tom Cruise and Jack Nicholson. It is a movie with a LOT of words. Aaron is famous for writing heavy scripts featuring 180 pages of dialogue when the average movie is usually around 120. In Aaron's case, shorter isn't always better. He argues in an episode of the West Wing that *"complexity is not a vice"*, believing that if you explain things to your audience properly, respecting their attention spans, you can get away with more than you think. What's next?

#**TEN**WORDS

THEODORE "TED" SORENSEN

"His text wasted no words. His delivery wasted no time".

When Ted Sorensen graduated from law school at the University of Nebraska, he had no legislative experience, no political experience and he had never written a speech – but that didn't stop Senator John F. Kennedy asking him to help with his Pulitzer prize winning book *Profiles in Courage* in 1955. Ted built up so much trust with Kennedy that just five short years later, Ted became not only Kennedy's closest advisor but the writer of the most famous inaugural address of all-time. Achieving such lofty status so early in your career would appeal to the ego of most young men, but not Ted. Supporting Kennedy as his most trusted advisor, he remained in the background, refusing to even take credit for his writing:

"If a man in high office speaks words which convey his principles and policies and ideas and he's willing to stand behind them and take whatever blame or therefore credit go with them, the speech is his".

If anyone understands the importance of communicating big ideas in small words and short sentences it is Ted Sorensen. Regarded as the best presidential speechwriter in history, he was JFK's closest advisor and the person who wrote the majority of his most memorable speeches. Sorensen's job was to distil JFK's messages down into short sentences and soundbites which the average person could understand, without diluting their meaning or significance.

READ: *White House Ghosts: Speech Writers* (2008)
WATCH: *JFK's Inauguration Speech* (1961)
FOLLOW: (... the speech transcript as you watch)

The secret to Sorensen's success as a speech writer was his insistence upon making Kennedy's speeches more than *"mere words"*. He hated claims that Kennedy was *"style over substance"* and as such made sure that every word was powerful, carefully chosen and perfectly placed. Ted made every speech 20-30 minutes and crowded them with so many facts that they would not allow for any excess of sentiment. *"His text wasted no words. His delivery wasted no time"*.

#**TEN**WORDS

KEVIN SPACEY

"The audience is the most important part of any story".

Too often we think that words aren't enough. If you trust the words, you'll start to discover the moments you need to actually emphasize". Speaking advice from the spaceman during one of his lessons on Masterclass.com.

If any of my presentations have ever successfully inspired or educated an audience, I have Kevin Spacey to thank for it. As a marketer, he blew my mind when I heard him speak at Content Marketing World in 2014, but the lessons he taught me during his Masterclass.com remain the single biggest reason why I love being in front of an audience so much. It's not always been that way. I was always the shyest kid at school and was terrified of public speaking. I still get nervous before a talk, but Kevin's Masterclass has shown me how to memorise a script, how to keep an audience interested, and most importantly how to involve the audience, giving them something useful to take away from every *"performance"*.

"Actors should be overheard, not listened to, because the audience is 50% of the performance".

Today, I often start my marketing presentations with the best piece of advice I received from Kevin after that content marketing gig in Cleveland: *"The story is everything, but you must remember that the audience is the most important part of the story. And it is your job to tell that story as fast and as compellingly as possible"*.

There are many things I forget when I'm presenting in front of a large audience, but as long as I remember that one piece of advice from the spaceman, I know I'll be OK.

READ: Kevin Spacey's Masterclass.com
WATCH: House of Cards
FOLLOW: @KevinSpacey

#**TEN**WORDS

KEVIN SPACEY

"When you've done well in business, it's your responsibility to send the elevator back down„.

*Advice **Jack Lemmon** gave Kevin Spacey about how we should all invest our time in the next generation.*

#TENWORDS

EVAN SPIEGEL

"Trading for some short term gain is not very interesting".

Evan Spiegel lives by three business rules and encourages other entrepreneurs to do the same:
1. Embrace what makes you different.
2. Honor those who will come after you.
3. Create something that you don't want to sell.

DOWNLOAD: Snapchat
WATCH: Evan Spiegel's USC Commencement Speech
FOLLOW: $SNAP

Snapchat founder Evan Spiegel is the reason that so many people are now *"telling stories in swipes"*. The app he created while at Stanford University in September 2011 now has over 160 million users and is redefining the way that younger generations are talking to each other and consuming news stories. Evan was not a great student. He was more focused on building Snapchat, the mobile messaging service where users can send texts, pictures and videos from one user to another with the option of having it disappear after 10 seconds. Evan loved the idea of telling stories quickly.

Originally called "*Picaboo*", the idea was to create a selfie app which allowed users to share images that were explicitly short-lived and self-deleting. The temporary nature of the pictures was supposed to encourage *"frivolity"* and emphasise a more natural flow of interaction. Evan was so convinced that his new form of storytelling would change the world that he even turned down an offer of $3 billion from Mark Zuckerberg to buy his app. Shocked and confused why a student would turn down such a ridiculous offer, a reporter from Forbes asked Evan what he was thinking? Evan replied, *"There are very few people in the world who get to build a business like this. Trading for some short-term gain is not very interesting."* Those last ten words certainly seem to be paying off. Snapchat went public in March 2017 with a valuation of $28 billion.

#**TEN**WORDS

EVAN SPIEGEL

We used to tell stories in **sentences.**

Today we tell stories in **swipes.**

#TENWORDS

STEVEN SPIELBERG

"I don't dream at night. I dream for a living".

Steven Spielberg has a problem. His imagination never turns off. "*I wake up so excited that I can't eat breakfast*", he said recently, "*I've never run out of energy*". Isn't that a wonderful thing to hear from someone who has been in the same job for over 38 years and still bounces out of bed to go to work. Granted, Spielberg does not have your average job, neither does he have your average salary, but he got to where he is by working hard. He had a loving but modest upbringing. His mother was a concert pianist and his dad was a computer engineer. Spielberg's first movie was about a train crash that he made with his model train set when he was 12. As a kid he couldn't think of anything more fun to do, so he took his father's movie camera and continued to make three or four-minute stories. His dream was to go to college to learn how to make movies. He applied to the University of Southern California (USC) School of Cinema Arts. He was rejected. Twice.

One of Spielberg's great skills is repurposing great stories, instead of insisting on original material. One of the reasons *Jaws* and *A.I.* were so successful for example is because they were just modern interpretations of *Moby Dick* and *Pinocchio*. Spielberg just re-mixed the stories and reinvented them with his own spin. Marketers, film makers and storytellers take note: you don't have to create original content all the time. You just have to tell a great story differently.

When Spielberg was 16 years old he wrote and created a sci-fi film called Firelight on a budget of just $500. The cast included his high school friends and he shot the movie in his garage. He even composed the film's score on clarinet himself. The movie was shown to an audience of 500 people who paid $1 each. One guest must have paid double because Spielberg came out of his debut with a profit of one dollar. Not a bad way to start your film making career.

READ: *Steven Spielberg* by Joseph McBride
WATCH: *Lincoln* by Steven Spielberg
FOLLOW: @DWanimation

#**TEN**WORDS

ANDREW STANTON

"Art is messy. Art is chaos. You need a system".

Andrew Stanton is the chief creative writer for Pixar behind their hit movies including Finding Nemo, WALL-E and Toy Story. The format he uses for writing his stories has been adopted not just by other screenwriters, but by business leaders, politicians and advertising executives. It even worked when I asked some IBM execs to use it as a model to re-write their PowerPoint presentations.

READ: *The Stoyteller's Secret* by Carmine Gallo
WATCH: Andrew Stanton's TED Talk
FOLLOW: @AndrewStanton | @Pixar

"*You had me at '**fish**'*" is precisely what John Lasseter, the co-founder of Pixar told writer-director Andrew Stanton following his exhaustive pitch for his '*passion project*'. That one word was enough for John to give the green light to Finding Nemo which went on to be the most popular DVD of all time selling over 40 million copies. Finding Nemo, just like Cars, Toy Story and WALL-E all followed the same formula.

We all know that any good story should have a beginning, a middle and an end, but few people know the exact template which the foundations for all these box office hits are based upon. So here it is, the 7-step process that all Pixar movies follow.

1. Once there was a _____.
   [A protagonist / hero with a goal is the most important element of a story.]
2. Every day here _____.
   [The hero's world must be in balance at the beginning.]
3. Until one day _____.
   [A compelling story introduces conflict].
4. Because of that _____.
   [This step separates a blockbuster from an average story because it keeps a cohesive flow in between scenes.]
5. Because of that _____.
6. Until finally _____.
7. Ever since then _____.
   [The moral of the story is.....]

Next time you write a story or need to give a speech or presentation, try it for yourself.

#**TEN**WORDS

JON STEWART

"Competence is a rare commodity in this day and age".

Jon Stewart is the benchmark upon which all chat show hosts on TV measure themselves. Turning a late night political satire show with low ratings, into one of America's most loved (and trusted) "news" shows, and keeping it *that good* for almost seventeen years, is one of the greatest accomplishments in the history of TV entertainment. His amazing ability to get to the heart of a subject by simplifying complicated political topics and making them funny launched him into the hearts and minds of his audience. (Comedians know that the fastest way to make someone remember something is to make them laugh). Under Jon's leadership over 17 years hosting The Daily Show has been voted one of the top 100 greatest TV shows of all time by TIME magazine, winning him 22 Emmy Awards in the process. But as Stewart himself likes to remind people (using ten words!) success didn't come easy:

"It took years of trying to become an overnight success".

Stewart started out as a stand-up comedian, playing several shows a night on New York's brutal comedy circuit, so he understands what hard work, dedication, and commitment to a project looks like. He was asked shortly before retiring from the Daily Show for the secret to his success. Especially in an era of 'fake news'. *"Love what you do and get good at it"* he replied, *"Competence is a rare commodity in this day and age".*

"If you're going to give people 20 minutes of news satire, you've also got to give them Tiffani-Amber Thiessen or you're going to have rioting in the streets".

Jon Stewart understands what his audience wants (and needs).

READ: *Angry Optimist* by Lisa Rogak
WATCH: Comedians in Cars with Jon Stewert
FOLLOW: @TheDailyShow

#**TEN**WORDS

JON STEWART

Between 1999 and 2015 Jon Stewart turned the daily show from a low ratings talk show to one of the most influential shows on US television. His secret to the success of the show was creating funny segments from short headlines. The Daily Show continues to lead the ratings on Comedy Central by talking about big ideas in small words and short funny sentences.

BIZ STONE

"There are more smart people out there than in here".

"It took Twitter ten years of hard work to become and overnight success. It is a triumph of humanity NOT technology. It's about people not the platform". @Biz

READ: Things a Little Bird Told Me by Biz Stone
WATCH: Any interview between @Jack and @Biz
FOLLOW: @Biz

In the early days of Twitter, Biz Stone (*one of the co-founders*) appointed himself the *Employee Happiness Officer*, making his main responsibility the task of educating and inspiring new recruits. Desperate to build a strong culture based on love, acceptance and harmony, Biz created an *"on-boarding"* program which he thought would do the trick. He based this program on *"6 Assumptions"* (averaging ten words each!) that would create happier employees and better working environments. I like to think of these *assumptions* as *"The 6 Rules for Building a Happy Company"*:

6 Rules For Building A Happy Company

1. We don't always know what's going to happen.
2. There are more smart people out there than in here.
3. We will win if we do the right thing for our users.
4. The only deal worth doing is a win-win deal.
5. Our coworkers are smart and they have good intentions.
6. We can build a business, change the world, and have fun.

Every company should have rules like these, especially the last one because we *all* need a purpose. We all need a good reason to bounce out of bed each morning. And we all want to enjoy our jobs *and* have fun, hopefully, while doing a little bit of good along the way.

#TENWORDS

BIZ STONE

After co-founders Ev, Jack, Noah and Biz decided against TWTTR as the name for their fledgling SMS powered update network, this was the first sketch of the UI for "Twitter" that Biz Stone drew in his notebook.

#**TEN**WORDS

LEVI STRAUSS

"I wanted to build an orphanage, not invent denim pants".

In 1849 Levi Straus travelled to San Francisco from New York to establish a dry goods business, hoping to profit from California's gold rush. This seemed like a good idea at the time until the huge influx of people hoping to seek their fortune forced the cost of living sky high. Levi soon discovered that he was unable to even sell a length of canvas for making tents. After brainstorming with his friend and tailor Jacob Davis, they decided to turn the rough fabric into ten pairs of working trousers for the miners. The pants sold well but they soon wore out due to the wear and tear that the miners and their tools subjected them to. Inspired by the metal rivets in his horse blanket, Jacob tried the horse rivets on Levi's pants and unwittingly created the first pair of riveted blue jeans in 1871. Convinced that this was an innovation worth investing in, Levi offered Jacob the $68 necessary to file the patent and so on May 20th, 1873, patent number 139121 was filed and Levi Strauss and Co. was born. Canvas was soon replaced by denim and an indigo dye was chosen to colour the pants as it was the cheapest dye on the market. The first profits from Levi's pants allowed him to donate $5 to the San Francisco Protestant Orphanage. Over the following years, profits from Levi's blue jeans allowed the company to sponsor the the Jewish shelter for orphaned children and pay for a new railway line, making public transport in San Francisco more affordable and accessible to everyone.

"I believe that you make your mark in the world not just by what you do, but also how you do it". Levi Strauss

READ: *Originals* by Adam Grant
WATCH: The 501® Jean: Stories of an Original
FOLLOW: @LeviStraussCo

#TENWORDS

VALENTINA TERESHKOVA

"Once you've been into space, you appreciate our fragile earth".

Valentina was the first woman in space. As her rocket launched into space she yelled into the intercom, Hello sky, take off your hat, I am on my way!". Valentina still sees her Vostok-6 occasionally in the centre for cosmonaut training. And every time she passes it by, she strokes it and says, 'My lovely one, my best and most beautiful friend".

READ: *Valentina Tereshkova* by Heather Feldman
WATCH: Vostok VI mission highlights on YouTube
FOLLOW: Your dreams.

When Valentina Tereshkova was a little girl she dreamed of exploring the world. Growing up in 1937 in Russia in a family that couldn't even afford bread forced her to comfort herself with stories and dreams, but unlike the other girls in her school, Valentina insisted that her dream would become real one day.

A few years later, when the space race between the United States and the USSR began, the USSR was desperate to be the first country to send a woman into space. There was no official space program for woman, so they turned to a parachute club, looking for women with the requisite skills to become cosmonauts. The training was gruelling and Valentina was up against five other tough women, but she wanted this opportunity so much more than the other girls that she worked harder than them all to secure her place. In 1963, two years after Yuri Gagarin's mission, Valentina became the first woman in space when she flew solo on a space shuttle called Vostok VI. She orbited the earth 48 times setting a new record, but the return flight encountered problems. Nauseated and disoriented Valentina manually fixed the problem just before she passed out. The photos that she took not only helped us gain a better understanding of earth's atmosphere but they helped her to inspire other women with her story when she returned home. Today Valentina is 80. Now she dreams of going to Mars!

#TENWORDS

PETER THIEL

"What one truth do most people disagree with you on?"

Almost everything Peter Thiel says is controversial. Cut from the same cloth as Elon Musk, Thiel wants to solve the world's biggest problems. But he's not referring to poverty, malaria or climate change ~ he wants to solve the problems of death and sleep. He is a firm believer that the first person who will live to be 1,000 is alive today. For this reason, he invests in people and technology that most other investors ignore, because the pay off may be too far into the future.

The first question that Thiel usually asks people seeking his investment or advice are these ten words. Like most of the statements in this book, it is a hugely complicated concept, hidden inside a short and simple sentence. The question itself forces you to think differently. It is also psychologically difficult because anyone trying to answer must say something she knows to be unpopular. *"Brilliant thinking is rare"* Thiel says, *"but courage is in even shorter supply than genius"*.

Peter Thiel is worth almost $3Bn. The co-founder of PayPal, he was also the first outside investor in Facebook and (controversially) one of the only Silicon Valley business leaders who supported Donald Trump during his campaign.

Thiel believes that startups should be solving BIG problems because the only way to succeed at scale is to become a monopoly in your industry. I encourage you to read his superb book Zero-to-One because he talks in detail about the biggest mistakes startups make and how to avoid them, because *"the quickest way to fail is to go for 1% of a billion dollar market"*.

READ: Zero-to-One
WATCH: Peter Thiel + Wired "Successful Businesses".
FOLLOW: @PeterThiel. *(Although he never tweets!)*

"If an entrepreneur cannot explain his idea in 10 words or less, I'm not interested and I'm not investing."

PETER THIEL

#**TEN**WORDS

ALAN TURING

"Science is a differential equation. Religion is a boundary condition".

Turing was the mathematician credited with ending World War II two years early, and saving millions of lives by breaking encrypted Nazi communications. He was a shy man with a bad stutter, which caused him to choose his words carefully. I imagine he thought *very* carefully before uttering his most famous words, *"Sometimes it is the people no one imagines anything of who do the things that no-one can imagine"*.

READ: *Computing Machinery and Intelligence* (1950)
WATCH: *The Imitation Game* (Benedict Cumberbatch)
FOLLOW: Mentions of #AlanTuring

Buried underneath a statue in the centre of Manchester, not far away from where I got my first job, lies an Amstrad CPC-464 like the one that I used to own in the 1980's. Sadly I wasn't the person to bury this particular computer. It was owned by Glyn Hughes, an artist from Lancashire who had been commissioned to create a sculpture which honoured the memory of Alan Turing. I loved that computer. And I love Alan Turing. My friends and I used to mention him all the time in computer club, remembering him as a local hero. He seemed like a regular guy, like one of us, but one who grew up to become the godfather of computer science and artificial intelligence. We all studied Turing's work on computing and AI and visited Bletchley to see the Bombe and the Enigma machine, but the thing I'll never forget is sitting in his chair in *"Hut 8"* and learning about his *seven* habits for productivity. Habits that Stephen Covey wishes he wrote, and habits that are just as relevant today as they were eighty years ago when he wrote them:

The 7 Productive Habits of Alan Turing
1. Try to see things as they are.
2. Don't get sidetracked by ideologies.
3. Be practical.
4. Break big problems down into smaller tasks.
5. Just keep going.
6. Be playful.
7. Remember that it is people who matter.

#**TEN**WORDS

MARK TWAIN

"Facts are stubborn things but statistics are much more pliable".

"Mark Twain carried with him a Webster's Unabridged Dictionary over mountain passes, across scorched deserts, and through land infested with bandits and Indians. He wanted to make himself a master of words, and with his characteristic courage and common sense, he set about doing the things necessary to bring that mastery about". Dale Carnegie

READ: *Roughing It* by Mark Twain
WATCH: *Mark Twain* (Documentary) on PBS
FOLLOW: @MarkTwain

Mark Twain lived a colourful life as a printer, riverboat pilot, journalist, travel writer and publisher. He was one of the finest wordsmiths the world has ever seen. I love the fact he cared about words *so much* that he insisted on taking his dictionary with him everywhere. But this was no pocket-sized book of words as we know today, this a was Webster's unabridged dictionary, containing almost half a million entries over 2,600 pages. Having a tome like that sat on your coffee table would have been impressive enough, but Twain travelled a lot. Living in Missouri, he often travelled 1,700 miles to Nevada by stagecoach, a journey which took him along cowboy trails beset by all kinds of danger. He was literally taking his life in his own hands. Speed and agility were crucial in navigating the trail as quickly and safely as possible. It was a notoriously slow trail with no access to food or fresh water for large parts of the journey, so all supplies had to be carried on board. Any additional weight could be the difference between safety and disaster, so baggage was charged by the ounce. The heavier the cargo, the higher the risk, the more money the drivers wanted. Despite all this, Twain insisted on carrying his huge dictionary with him, paying for words by the ounce! I wonder what he would have made of the smartphone, where despite having the entire world's knowledge constantly in our pockets, we still mostly ignore it in favour of swiping right and retweeting fake news.

#**TEN**WORDS

MARK TWAIN

SORRY I WROTE YOU SUCH A LONG LETTER...

"I notice that you use plain, simple language, short words and brief sentences. That is the way to write English - it is the modern way and the best way. Stick to it; don't let fluff and flowers and verbosity creep in.

When you catch an adjective, kill it. No, I don't mean utterly, but kill most of them - then the rest will be valuable. They weaken when they are close together. They give strength when they are wide apart. An adjective habit, or a wordy, diffuse, flowery habit, once fastened upon a person, is as hard to get rid of as any other vice".

Mark Twain to D. W. Bowser, 20 March 1880

#TENWORDS

GARY VAYNERCHUK

"Put out quality content every day and *engage* around it".

The best advice Gary ever gave to me was that *"the future belongs to the DJ's"*. Too many people have become obsessed with creating original content or waiting to have a unique idea, instead what they should be doing is re-mixing existing ideas and presenting them to new audiences in ways which they haven't seen before.

READ: *Crush It* by Gary Vaynerchuk
WATCH: Gary's Keynote at Inc 500 (2011)
FOLLOW: @GaryVee

Gary Vaynerchuk was the first person I ever followed on Twitter. I discovered him through his WineLibraryTV show, not because I was particularly interested in wine, but because he was clearly doing something revolutionary and I wanted to witness it. Back in a time when people were still figuring out whether they should be blogging, and long before we even know what a YouTube vlogger was, Gary launched a video blog. It was a blog where he talked about some of the wines he was selling from his father's business. But these weren't any wines. Some of them were $12,500 per case vintage wines. So, not the kind of wine's you'd expect to see hawked by a foul-mouthed New Yorker, on a homemade video blog filmed on a $200 Flipcam in one take. But that's exactly what Gary did.

Filming an "episode" of WineLibraryTV at 9am each morning, Gary filmed himself talking to the camera in one shot of between 10 and 20 minutes and uploaded it (un-edited) to Viddler with basic graphics and hyperlinks by 11am. He did that every day for over 1,000 episodes and with only word of mouth for promotion, Vaynerchuk grew the business from $3 million to $60 million a year within 5 years. In August 2011, Vaynerchuk stepped away from WineLibraryTV to build the social media agency VaynerMedia with his brother AJ. VaynerMedia is currently one of the world's largest specialist social media agencies.

#**TEN**WORDS

CEDRIC VILLANI

"To achieve good results, work all night and eat soup".

In 2010, Cedric Villani was awarded the Fields Medal. The Fields Medal is like the Nobel prize for mathematics. Only it's only handed out every 4 years. To people under 40. And if the entries are not good enough, it's not handed out at all. So winning one is a big deal. Cedric Villani is a very big deal. Through his talks and his unique perspective of numbers, he is one of the reasons many school kids are falling in love with maths.

READ: *Birth of a Theorem* by Cedric Villani.
WATCH: *"What's So Sexy About Math?"* TED Talk.
FOLLOW: Cedric's work at Marie Curie University.

Cedric Villani is the Lady Gaga of Mathematics. Both hugely talented and beautifully eccentric, Villani is making maths relevant to an audience of people who weren't previously interested in numbers. He never intended to become famous or spend his younger days dreaming about winning the highest accolade in mathematics. It all happened by accident. One day Cedric needed to write a course. He expected it to be around one hundred pages, so he started writing. Before long he felt like some of the sources weren't as credible as they could be, so he started to rework the research. Many of the articles needed rewriting and before long, he had ended up rewriting the entire course from scratch. He kept rewriting his work until each chapter was "*singing*" to him.

Finally, after years of working day and night, the course was finally complete and Cedric felt happy with his work. The first time he read it all the way through, he made sure he had no distractions. So he took a week off, went to the market for vegetables and made a huge pot of soup, bought lots of bread, and ate nothing else for a week. He stayed up day and night revising and editing his work. Without realising it, he had rewritten proofs on differential equations and mathematical physics that had never been done before. When asked how he did it, he replied with these ten words: *"To achieve good results, work all night and eat soup"*.

#**TEN**WORDS

DITA VON TEESE

"Only mediocrity is safe from ridicule. Dare to be different".

"Heels and red lipstick will put the fear of god into people". Dita Von Teese is an American burlesque dancer, vedette, glamour model, costume designer, entrepreneur and actress. She re-invented burlesque performance with her memorable 1940's vintage inspired shows, and once appeared at a benefit for the New York Academy of Art wearing nothing but $5 million worth of diamonds!

READ: *Your Beauty Mark* by Dita Von Teese
WATCH: *The Death of Salvador Dali* by Delaney Bishop
FOLLOW: @DitaVonTeese

Dita Von Teese is an evangelist. But not an evangelist like me who speaks at conferences about technology. And she's certainly not an evangelist like you might find in a church. Dita Von Teese is a *"glamour evangelist"*. "*I am a 'glamour evangelist' and yes, I may take it a bit too far sometimes but sometimes you just need to be willing to try new things.*" Dita Von Teese has built her career upon trying new things and often going a bit too far. From modeling for Playboy to acting, from burlesque dancing to fashion design, the 44-year-old entrepreneur has become a major force in the world of lingerie design and is "*trying to remind people what glamour really means*".

Dita thinks "*For some [glamour] may be private jets and wealth and Louis Vuitton or all these things, but glamour is walking into a room and people wanting to know more about you and creating a mystique. We can be whoever we want to be and you don't have to lament what you weren't born with*" Dita told News.com.au. "*Most celebrities travel with a 'glam squad', and that's totally respectable, but I really want to encourage and inspire woman to put it in their everyday life*". She doesn't want to change the world and she doesn't pretend that what she is doing has any deep meaning or higher purpose. She just wants people to change themselves to be happier and more self-confident. But as missions go, that's still a pretty good one.

#TENWORDS

JOHNNIE WALKER

"I am a slow Walker. But I never walk backwards".

John Walker was just 14 when his father died in 1819, leaving him £417 in a trust. Determined that he would spend his time more wisely that working in the fields like the other boys his age, the trustees were tasked with helping John to invest the money in building a store which served the local community. True to his wishes, John and the trustees opened a grocers on the High Street in Kilmarnock, but this wasn't just any grocers, this was an Italian warehouse, grocery, and wine and spirits shop (a revolutionary concept back in 1820). Building the business was tough and the unpredictable Scottish weather constantly disrupted deliveries, but it was the whisky that kept people coming back to John's shop. The only problem was consistency.

Making a single malt was a tricky process. One month the flavours were great, the next they could be unpalatable, so Johnnie (as he was known to his friends and family) decided to create his own whisky. One that could guarantee consistency by being blended from different batches, not a single malt. Perfecting the blending process was a slow and frustrating process but Johnnie Walker refused to give up. He told his customers, *"I am a slow Walker. But I never walk backwards"*. Committed to creating the perfect blend which satisfied the palettes of his customers, Johnnie eventually settled on a *"Kilmarnock Blend"*. It wasn't long before word of this smooth and consistent blend

READ: Johnnie Walker Wikipedia page
WATCH: *"Keep Walking"* BBH ad with Robert Carlyle
FOLLOW: ... in Johnnies footsteps and *"Keep Walking"*.

#TENWORDS

JOHNNIE WALKER

1908   2015

spread fast among the local community and the Kilmarnock Blend Whisky officially became *"Johnnie Walker Whisky"*. The store continued to grow, serving the Scottish community with all their household essentials and by the time of his death in 1857, whisky was accounting for a large percentage of sales. Talking over the business was John's son Alexander Walker and his grandson Alexander Walker II.

Determined to extend John's legacy, the Alexander's committed to take the Johnnie Walker name even further a field. Their masterplan was to convince captains of Glasgow's trading ships to act as agents for him, taking Johnnie Walker whiskey to whatever port they were about to set sail. The whisky fast became an even bigger success, but smashed bottles onboard the ships became a problem and so the square bottle was created in order to minimise breakages. In another act of marketing genius, the Alexander's also slanted the label by 24°, allowing them to use a slightly larger font size for their father's name, making it stand out even more alongside other bottles. They even commissioned Tom Browne, the most sought after illustrator of his day, to reproduce a drawing of John Walker. Tom obliged, and over a whisky, he drew the now iconic 'Striding figure' device which graces the label of every Johnnie Walker bottle.

The brand grew consistently over the next eighty-years but by 1999, the Johnnie Walker label was struggling.

Global sales were down 14% showing no signs of improving and tough international markets were taking their toll. The whisky needed a consistent message, one which transcended cultural and international boundaries, so the brand's owners Diageo turned to their ad agency Bartle Bogle Hegarty for help. Recognising that they needed to rediscover what made Johnnie Walker special in the first place, BBH went back to Johnnie's original notebooks for inspiration. It was there that they stumbled across John's favourite ten word quote *"I am a slow Walker. But I never walk backwards"*. It was in that moment that the "Keep Walking" advertising campaign was launched. This was Johnnie Walker's first international ad campaign with a consistent message, and it couldn't have been any more perfect.

Many beautifully crafted TV spots and well written press ads later, Johnnie Walker is now the number one selling Scotch whisky in the world, shifting 19 million cases in 180 countries. Johnnie would no doubt be proud of his brand's success, but he would probably be even more proud that his motto *"Keep Walking"* is regularly credited in parliamentary speeches across the world wherever politicians are campaigning for a consistent message to help local communities.

#**TEN**WORDS

JEREMY WAITE

"I want to _____
in order to _____
because if I don't _____".

Writing this book has been a cathartic process. It has also been a lot of fun. But more importantly, it has challenged me to find meaning in my marketing. Doing stuff is easy. Doing stuff that has a purpose is hard. But finding your purpose, and understanding the consequences of not acting upon it, is really hard. That's why I was excited to write this book. So excited in fact that I wrote the whole thing in one hundred days.

READ: Jeremy.live
WATCH: Jeremy speak @IBM.
FOLLOW: @JeremyWaite

In 2005 I owned a design agency called Juicy. I had a business plan, an elevator pitch and an impressive list of open minded clients who trusted us with their corporate identity. I was convinced I would win some awards and cement our position as one of the exciting new agencies to watch. The only problem was that my elevator pitch only consisted of ten words: "*We are the UK's most exciting and ethical design agency*". We had a plan but we didn't have a purpose, even though I knew deep down that good design and marketing should do a lot more than just "*sell more stuff*".

Sadly, Juicy ended up filing for bankruptcy in 2008 but it was years later before I fully understood why. I was good at explaining what I wanted to do, but I didn't think deeply enough about *why* I was doing it or what I had to lose. I also didn't understand that '*what you stand for is more important than what you sell*'. (It didn't help that my business partner disappeared overnight either). So after many late nights, whiskeys and scribbles on the back of napkins, I came up with these ten words as a structure to make sure that I didn't make the same mistake again. Today, I am driven by a desire to encourage others to do more meaningful work as they to build their own ventures and careers. That's why I wrote Ten Words. Try filling in the gaps yourself. It's *really* hard, and it takes a lot of time to fill it in properly. But I promise you it's time well spent.

#TENWORDS

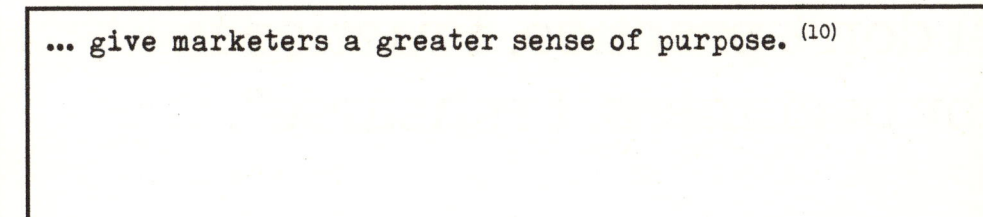

I want to...

... give marketers a greater sense of purpose. (10)

in order to...

... make a meaningful difference to global brands. (10)

because if I don't...

we're just selling people *more stuff* (10)'..

#TENWORDS

YUJA WANG

"I don't practice. Practice is for beginners. I rehearse".

Yuja Wang is a cultural ambassador for Rolex and Red Bull. She is arguably the best classical pianist in the world today known for her *"blistering technique"*. Yuja *"rehearses"* for six hours each day.

READ: *"Yuja Wang: Art of Performance"* New Yorker
WATCH: *Yuja Wang Dresses Up Chopin* by Red Bull
FOLLOW: @YujaWang

One of the best pieces of presenting advice I ever received was from Tony Robbins. He told me *"Don't practice until you get it right, practice until you never get it wrong"*. Often the best performers look natural and supremely confident, but they come across that way because of the endless hours they invested in perfecting their craft. Superstar pianist Yuja Wang doesn't practice. She rehearses. I had the pleasure of seeing her perform at London's Southbank Centre in early 2017 and she was incredible. No sheet music. No lighting effects. No dramatic entrance. No glitz. And the only glamour was her amazing dress. Her entire performance took everyone's breath away. She didn't even speak one word to the audience, letting her music do the talking for her.

Yuja takes a lot of criticism in the classical music world, due to the short tight dresses that she wears. She says she just dresses like a twenty-something when she's 40 she'll dress differently. But Yuja has very carefully crafted her image to make her memorable because she understands that when such a petite woman takes to the stage and plays with immense power, the juxtaposition is all the more dramatic. It raises an age old marketing debate about packaging and substance: if the content is poor, it doesn't matter how amazing the packaging is. But if the packaging is beautiful and the content exceeds all expectations, then what you have is rather special. Yuja Wang is rather special.

"Preach the Gospel at all times. Use words if necessary."

ST. FRANCIS of ASSISI

#**TEN**WORDS

ANDY WARHOL

"In the future, everyone will be famous for 15 minutes".

"People should fall in love with their eyes closed".

Andy Warhol told stories with a silkscreen. His iconic prints of Coca-Cola bottles, Marilyn Monroe and Campbell's Soup tins are recognised all over the world. In 2013 his *Silver Car Crash* sold at Sotherby's for $105.4 million.

READ: *The Philosophy of Andy Warhol* by Himself
WATCH: *Chelsea Girls* by Andy Warhol
VISIT: Any gallery showing his original artwork

When Andy Warhol first uttered those ten words early in 1960 at the beginning of the Pop Art movement, little did he know how prophetic those words would become. In a world obsessed with fans, followers and subscribers - selfies, stardom and status, *"we"* have provided a platform for thousands of the most unqualified and untalented people to have their fifteen minutes of fame.

"Being good in business is the most fascinating kind of art".

I love Warhol because he made no apologies for being a commercial artist. He wanted his art to tell provocative stories, using the mediums of print, film and books to curate his opinions on topics such as celebrity, advertising, sex and the role of the media. He was a great artist and a truly unique character who pioneered a new movement in the art world, but he wasn't an artist in the purest sense of the word. He built *"The Factory"* in Mid-town Manhattan, a commercial studio where his staff could mass-produce his artworks, telling journalists and art critics that, *"Pop art is for everyone"*. He wanted his art to be accessible, not exclusive, so he regularly hosted parties in *The Factory* for friends such as David Bowie, Bob Dylan, Lou Reed, Grace Jones and Debby Harry. Warhol's factory is now the model used by all commercial celebrity *"artists"* such as Damien Hirst, Banksy, Tom Ford and (Blur album designer) Julian Opie.

#**TEN**WORDS

ANDY WARHOL

STOP MAKING STUPID PEOPLE FAMOUS

#**TEN**WORDS

ANDY WARHOL

#**TEN**WORDS

ANDY WARHOL

"What's great about this country is that America started the tradition where the richest consumers buy essentially the same things as the poorest. You can be watching TV and see Coca-Cola, and you know that the President drinks Coca-Cola, Liz Taylor drinks Coca-Cola, and just think, you can drink Coca-Cola, too.

A Coke is a Coke and no amount of money can get you a better Coke than the one the bum on the corner is drinking. All the Cokes are the same and all the Cokes are good. Liz Taylor knows it, the President knows it, the bum knows it, and you know it".

#**TEN**WORDS

THOMAS J. WATSON Sr.

"Double your rate of failure, that's where you'll find success".

"All the problems of the world could be settled easily if men were only willing to think. The trouble is that men very often resort to all sorts of devices in order not to think because thinking is such hard work". Thomas J. Watson Jr.

READ: *Father, Son & Co* by Thomas J. Watson Jr.
WATCH: *Hidden Figures* by Theodore Melfi
FOLLOW: @IBMWatson

As an evangelist at IBM, I talk a lot about the success and innovations I see at the world's sixth largest brand. The company has thousands of engineers who are paid to play with technology, invent new things, and find solutions for some of the world's biggest problems. But it is not the success of IBM which inspires me the most. It is its failure. IBM has failed a lot. And will continue to fail a lot. Whether developing new products, re-inventing or re-organising itself, IBM does it's best to double its failure rate, because it knows that's where success will come from.

Thomas J. Watson Sr. knew a thing or two about failure. Watson first tried his hand at teaching but quit after the first day saying it was not for him. He then took a course in accounting and business before getting his first 'real' job as a book keeper on $6 a week. After a year he became a travelling salesman peddling organs and pianos around the farming community on $10 per week, but he realised he would be earning $70 per week if he were on a commission, so he quit to move to the City of Buffalo hoping to make his fortune. After a brief but unsuccessful period selling sewing machines, Watson tried selling shares, but his boss was a showman renowned for his disreputable conduct and absconded with the commission and the loan funds. Next Watson opened a butchers shop in Buffalo. Sadly that soon failed as well, leaving Watson with no money, no investment, and no job.

THOMAS J. WATSON Sr.

But the one thing he had left in his butchers shop was a newly acquired NCR cash register, for which he had to arrange the transfer of the instalment to the shop's new owner. Upon visiting NCR, Watson organized the paper work and asked their local sales manager John J. Range for a job. Determined to join the company, Watson repeatedly called on Range until, after a number of failed attempts, he was finally hired as a sales apprentice.

At the time, NCR was a leading sales organization with a sales and management style that other companies wanted to copy. At first, Watson was a poor salesman, but Range took him under his wing and mentored him personally. Within a year Watson became the most successful salesman in the East, earning $100 per week and within four years he was assigned the task of rescuing an ailing division of the business in Rochester, New York. He was to receive an unprecedented 35% commission and reported directly to board of NCR. Watson turned the business around so successfully that NCR became a monopoly in the industry. Disrupting the industry took its toll, competitors sued, and long court cases ensued. The organization ran five divisions of the company at the time, so the executives decided to simplify things by forming one company, the Computer Tabulating Recording Company.

Watson was general manager and the president when the five companies merged with 1,300 employees. Eleven months later he was made president and within four years revenues had been doubled to $9 million, but the watershed moment came in 1924 when Watson renamed CTR as International Business Machines. At the time, IBM owned and leased to its customers more than 90 percent of all tabulating machines in the United States. When Watson died in 1956, IBM's revenues were $897 million, and the company had 72,500 employees. Not bad for someone who failed at teaching, butcherie and his first few sales jobs. Today IBM has 380,000 employees and sales of around $82 Billion. The company is still asking people to think differently and fail faster.

#**TEN**WORDS

#**TEN**WORDS

"We live in a society that doesn't like to think."

THOMAS J. WATSON Sr.

#TENWORDS

BILL WATTERSON

"A job title and salary don't measure a human's worth".

"The surest sign that intelligent life exists elsewhere in the universe is that it has never tried to contact us".
Bill Watterson

Calvin and Hobbes is one of the most loved comic strips in the world. It could also have been one of the most commercially successful strips in the world but its creator Bill Watterson never signed away the rights to anyone to make official merchandise (despite many lucrative multi-million dollar offers). Bill believes that what he stands for is more important than what he sells. He felt that licensed products violated *"the spirit of the strip"*, contradicted its message, and took him away from the work he loved. Bill never wanted to compromise the integrity of his work by finding Calvin on a Happy Meal box or seeing Hobbes on a box of cereal. At one point, both Steven Spielberg *and* George Lucas reached out asking to meet with Bill, but the artist, who felt schmoozing and publicity took his focus away from the strip, politely declined. Bill always said that *"letting your mind play is the best way to solve problems"*, a process which he says has helped him to make his best decisions.

"Money won't buy happiness but it will pay the salaries of a large research staff to study the problem".

Still, Bill hasn't done too badly by sticking to his principles and never *"selling out"*. To date, he has sold over 45 million books and continues to live privately (in Chagrin Falls, Ohio) away from the spotlight, hopefully, happy in the knowledge that his stories have brought joy to so many people.

READ: *Calvin & Hobbes* by Bill Watterson
WATCH: *Dear Mr. Watterson*
FOLLOW: @CalvinandHobbes

#**TEN**WORDS

BILL WATTERSON

> GIVEN THE PACE OF TECHNOLOGY, I PROPOSE WE LEAVE MATH TO THE MACHINES AND GO PLAY OUTSIDE.

#**TEN**WORDS

JOSIAH WEDGWOOD

"Beautiful forms are not made by chance at small expense".

Josiah Wedgwood revolutionising the way that pottery was manufactured and "brand marketing" was done. He pioneered direct mail, money back guarantees, self-service, free delivery, buy one get one free, and illustrated catalogues. It is perhaps fitting therefore that Josiah's great grandson was a gentleman explorer and anthropologist called Charles Darwin, who started a revolution of his own, with his *survival of the fittest* theory outlined in *"Origin of the Species"*.

READ: *Josiah Wedgwood* by Brian Dolan
WATCH: *Josiah Wedgwood: The Genius*
FOLLOW: @Wedgwood

Wedgwood Pottery was founded in 1759 by Josiah Wedgwood, in Stoke-on-Trent, close to where I used to work at Phones 4U. You may be familiar with the iconic Wedgwood blue and white relief patterns, but you may not be familiar with the fact that they were arguably the world's first *"brand"*. Long before Henry Ford became famous for automating his factory production line, Josiah Wedgwood figured out how to mass produce pottery in his Staffordshire based factory in the North of England. Unsure of how to promote his new company he gave it away for free to the royal family, through his family connections.

It took six years of what we now call *"product placement"* and *"influencer campaigns"*, but the powder blue Wedgwood earthenware was eventually noticed by the British Queen consort Charlotte of Mecklenberg-Strelitz, who gave her permission to call it *"Queen's Ware"*. With this seal of royal approval, Wedgwood created possibly the world's first branded direct mail campaign to raise awareness of his aspirational new brand. Ex-Burberry CEO Angela Ahrendts (now Apple's Head of Retail) deserves some credit for the term *"mass-market luxury"*, but Josiah Wedgwood was doing this 256 years ago. Wedgwood didn't just revolutionise the pottery industry, he became one of the founding fathers of the marketing industry and changed the way that companies spoke to their customers.

#TENWORDS

JOSIAH WEDGWOOD & SONS LTD.
ETRURIA
STOKE-ON-TRENT.

ESTABLISHED IN 1759 BY JOSIAH WEDGWOOD, F.R.S.

Manufacturers of
CHINAWARE, QUEENSWARE, GENERAL EARTHENWARE,
JASPERWARE BLACK BASALT, &C.

TRADE MARKS

WEDGWOOD
for China.

Original Registered Trade Mark
for Earthenware and Jasper
in use since 1760
WEDGWOOD

WORKS AND SHOWROOMS
ETRURIA, STOKE-ON-TRENT.

LONDON SHOWROOMS
MR FELTON WREFORD.
26-27 HATTON GARDEN.
HOLBORN CIRCUS, E.C.1.
FRANCE, BELGIUM &C.
MR CECIL HAVEN.
HOLLAND & SCANDINAVIA
MR F.L. THORLEY.
SOUTH AFRICA
MR R.L. HUTTY.
HULSTANS BUILDINGS.
SMITH STREET.
DURBAN.

NEW YORK SHOWROOMS
JOSIAH WEDGWOOD & SONS (INC)
MR K.L. WEDGWOOD, PRESIDENT.
255 FIFTH AVENUE.
SOUTH AMERICA
MR A.A. BAYAN.
CERRITO 776.
BUENOS AIRES.
AUSTRALASIA
MR J.W. ROBERTS.
99 QUEEN VICTORIA BUILDINGS.
GEORGE STREET.
SYDNEY. N.S.W.

Wedgwood was the first company (as far as I'm aware) to run a direct mail marketing campaign, in England in the late 17th century. Wedgwood are also credited with running the world's first influencer campaign with their *'Queensware'* and for creating the retail store layout that Apple uses today for its flagship stores.

#**TEN**WORDS

JOSIAH WEDGWOOD

WEDGWOOD STORE, LONDON *(1774)*
A cathedral to showcase "mass-market luxury" designed by creative director and industrial designer John Flaxman. Open spaces. Ornate pillars. A counter staffed by product experts and craftsmen. One of the most profitable retail spaces in London.

APPLE STORE, PARIS *(2009)*
A cathedral to showcase "mass-market luxury" designed by creative director and industrial designer Jonny Ive. Open spaces. Ornate pillars. Genius bar staffed by product experts. Apple is worlds most profitable retailer (per square foot).

#**TEN**WORDS

JOSIAH WEDGWOOD

"Beautiful forms and compositions are not made by chance, nor can they ever, in any material, be made at small expense.

A composition for cheapness and not excellence of workmanship is the most frequent and certain cause of the rapid decay and entire destruction of arts and manufactures„.

Josiah Wedgwood was the Steve Jobs of his day. Even the language he uses here sounds like something Steve might have said in a WWDC keynote.

#TENWORDS

ORSON WELLES

"I started at the top and worked my way down".

In 1941 Orson Welles co-wrote, produced, directed, and starred in *Citizen Kane* - one of the finest and most innovative films of all time. He regularly tops the list of the best directors of all time. Sadly, and somewhat bizarrely, Welles' first film was his finest work winning him an Oscar, but he never achieved anything like that success with subsequent films. But speak to any filmmaker about how to they learned to edit and tell technically better stories, they will point you towards one of Orson Welles movies. What made Welles such a great storyteller was that his stories were never linear. He cut many stories together into the same film and jumped between them at the height of each scene. Many writers use *"and then"* as they link one story to another, but not Orson Welles. He always used *"therefore"* and *"but"* to introduce drama and conflict such as *"therefore this happened..... BUT then this happened...!!!"*

Orson Welles started his career by creating his masterpiece Citizen Kane, but sadly ended in a darker place with him living off a daily diet of two rare steaks and a pint of scotch. Fittingly for this book, when a journalist asked him what word should be used to describe him towards the end of his life, he didn't reply with one, he replied with ten (taken from his most famous film): *"I don't think any word can explain a man's life".*

This emotional method of storytelling has been adopted by everyone from Hitchcock and Pixar to TV scriptwriters and 'mad men'. Although I did see an ad for an agency recently that said *"We value the customer, AND we always respect your budget, AND we have on-time delivery, AND..."* That's just lazy writing. It's not storytelling because there is no *"causality"*. No *"action-reaction"*. No *"but"*. Whether it's a film script *or* a corporate ad, we *need* to inject more drama into our sentences. We need more *"buts"*.

READ: *This is Orson Welles* by Orson Welles
WATCH: *Citizen Kane* by Orson Welles
LEARN: *F for Fake*: How to Structure a Video Essay

ORSON WELLES

*** THE SIX RULES OF WRITING ***

1. Never use a metaphor, simile, or other figure of speech which you are used to seeing in print.

2. Never use a long word where a short one will do.

3. If it is possible to cut a word out, always cut it out.

4. Never use the passive where you can use the active.

5. Never use a foreign phrase, a scientific word, or a jargon word if you can think of an everyday English equivalent.

6. Break any of these rules sooner than say anything outright barbarous.

ORSON WELLES (1946)

#TENWORDS

ERIC WEINSTEIN

"General fame is overrated. It's better to handpick your audience".

Eric Weinstein is MD of Thiel Capital, a PhD in mathematical physics from Harvard and a research fellow at the Mathematical Institute of Oxford University. He's a smart guy who finds nothing more exciting than a blank whiteboard. He writes the kind of research you *should* read.

READ: *Tools of Titans* by Tim Ferriss
WATCH: Eric Weinstein on *The Rubin Report*
FOLLOW: @EricRWeinstein

I've never had any desire to be famous, nor have I ever obsessed about how many thousand people follow me on social media, but I have always been curious about the actual value of a social audience and what influence they may (*or may not*) have. So when I heard Tim Ferriss interview Eric Weinstein on his podcast about social *"success"*, his ten words really struck a chord with me, *"General fame is overrated. It's better to handpick your audience"*.

"General fame is overrated" Weinstein explained. *"What you actually want is to be famous to 2,000 to 3,000 people that you handpick"*. Mainstream fame, he suggested, brings more liabilities than benefits, especially to business people. But if for example, you are known and respected by a few thousand high-caliber people (eg. The live TED audience) you will be able to do pretty much everything that you ever want to do in life. That size of audience provides maximum upside and minimal downside. I like to think of this as *"the law of small numbers"*. I have over 100,000 followers on twitter (*most of them seem to be either fake or bots*) but about 2,500 of them are *engaged* followers who I know and have a meaningful relationship with on some level. So to me, my Twitter community is actually the 2,500 people who care about the same stuff I do, not the other 97,500 who just make me look like an "*influencer*". To most people, I'm really not influential at all.

#**TEN**WORDS

ERIC WEINSTEIN

"Whenever you find yourself on the side of the majority, it is time to pause and reflect„.

#TENWORDS

MAE WEST

"I'm a woman of few words but lots of action".

When the Beatles asked permission to use a picture of West on the Sgt. Pepper's Lonely Hearts Band album cover, she replied, "*What would I be doing in a lonely hearts club?*"

If you've ever wondered where the Coca-Cola bottle got its contours from, look no further than Mae West. She first began performing professionally as a vaudeville act in 1907 (aged 14), but by the time she was 42 she was the highest-paid star in Hollywood and the second highest paid person in the United States. During that golden age of movies, women were expected to be seen but not *"involved"*, certainly not in the film making process anyway. But Mae West was never one for conformity and she had no interest in just reading lines (she wrote nine of the thirteen films in which she starred).

It all started when she re-wrote her first role in *Night After Night* in 1932 and stole the show, developing such a skill for writing memorable lines in short sentences that she soon became known as the queen of the double entendre. Mae West loved words, so much so that she wanted control over which ones she said on screen. As soon as she could, she insisted on having complete creative control over her own material, writing much of her own dialogue. There is nothing unusual about this today, but it was unheard of back in the early days of cinema for a woman to have creative control over her own words. "*The secret of it is to keep everything moving*", Mae said of her writing, "*Don't let the audience think of the dishes. You need to have some lines they can take away, like songs they go away humming*".

READ: Goodness Had Nothing To Do With It
WATCH: She Done Him Wrong with Cary Grant
FOLLOW: Her example. (Where appropriate).

#TENWORDS

Dame VIVIENNE WESTWOOD

"Buy less. Choose well. Make it last. Quality, not quantity".

"The sexiest people are thinkers". Dame Vivienne Westwood

Vivienne Westwood is a remarkable woman. She juggles the seemingly contradictory roles of world-renowned fashion designer, with being an impassioned, outspoken (and eccentric) environmental activist. Since igniting the punk movement with ex-partner and Sex Pistols' manager Malcolm McLaren, Dame Vivienne Westwood has been redefining British fashion for over 40 years. She is responsible for creating many of the most distinctive looks of our time. Yet at 76 Vivienne feels compelled to use her position in the limelight to address environmental issues, rather than focusing on designing and selling her clothes.

For Vivienne what she stands for is more important than what she sells, telling anyone who will listen that everyone is buying far too many clothes these days, and emblazons such remarks on her clothes during her London Fashion Week shows. Not what you would expect from a commercial designer whose very success lies in the quantity of her sales, not in the quality of her words. But then again, Vivienne has never been your average fashion designer. Neither has she ever been particularly driven by commercial success, other than being able to use it as a platform to communicate her ideals and values. So the next time you see a Westwood t-shirt with Vivienne's favourite ten words on it, think about what it means. This is no marketing slogan or provocative sales campaign. She means it.

READ: *Get a Life: The Diaries of Vivienne Westwood*
WATCH: *Westwood* by Lorna Tucker
FOLLOW: @VivienneWestwood on Instgram

#TENWORDS

ROBIN WILLIAMS

"Anything *not* funny, at a certain point, *will* be funny".

"No matter what anybody else tells you, words and ideas can change the world. We don't read and write poetry because it's cute. We read and write poetry because we are members of the human race. And the human race is filled with passion. Medicine, law business, engineering, these are noble pursuits and necessary to sustain life. But poetry, beauty, romance, love, these are what we stay alive for".

WATCH: Mork & Mindy
WATCH: Dead Poets Society
WATCH: Good Will Hunting

When I was young and impressionable, I watched the movie Wall Street and decided that I wanted to work on the stock exchange. The idea of being Gordon Gekko, working in a fast paced industry and wearing red braces appealed to me. Or it did at least, until I realised that I preferred working with people more than numbers, I didn't want to burn out at 25 and I didn't look good in red braces after all. I also watched Dead Poets Society in 1989, a film which was single handedly responsible for making me fall in love with poetry and the art of storytelling. *"Carpe diem"**, despite feeling like a bit of a cliché these days, remain my two favourite words.

"No matter what people tell you, words and ideas can change the world".

The person I have to thank for this, of course, is Robin Williams. A brilliant man who was as much a writer as he was a performer. I first discovered Williams, like many did, as he rose to stardom with the spectacularly bizarre and zany *Mork & Mindy* show. I thought he was hilarious but I was always more inspired by the deeper roles he played in his most iconic film roles, as John Keating in Dead Poets Society and Sean Maguire in Good Will Hunting — two of my all-time favourite films. He was a brilliantly beautiful man. And the world is a much sadder place without him in it.

Rest in peace *O' Captain, My Captain*.

* *Carpe Diem* is Latin for *Seize the Day*

Carpe Diem.

JOHN KEATING

#TENWORDS

JOHN "JOCKO" WILLINK

"Good".

"Jocko" Willink is a podcaster, author and retired United States Navy SEAL. He received the Silver Star and Bronze Star for his service in the Iraq War and was commander of SEAL Team Three's Task Unit Bruiser during the Battle of Ramadi. You should check out his superb TEDx talk about *"Extreme Ownership"*.

READ: Extreme Ownership by Jocko Willink
LISTEN: The Jocko Willink Podcast
FOLLOW: @JockoWillink

This is a book about ten words. Many of the people I have written about made a name for themselves one way or another through their ten word mantras and philosophies. But not everyone needs ten words. Especially not Jocko Willink. Why use ten words when one will do? Because if you are a commander of a Navy SEAL unit operating in hostile areas, speed and brevity are of utmost importance. A few extra words could delay your action under fire by a few critical seconds, and be the difference between life and death. As a result, *"Jocko"* became a man of few words, notorious for saying *"Good"*, especially when things were going wrong. Jocko believes that when anything is going bad, there is always going to be some good that comes from it.

- *"Didn't get promoted?"* **Good**. (More time to get better).
- *"Mission got cancelled?"* **Good**. (We can focus on another one).
- *"Got beat?"* **Good**. (You learned).
- *"Unexpected problems?"* **Good**. (We have the opportunity to figure out a solution).

After a while, Jocko's men stopped asking him questions because his response was always *"Good"*. One day one of his team challenged him saying that things were *not* good. *"No"*, Jocko replied. *"Because no matter what is happening, if you can still say the word 'Good', it means that you're still alive. And you can still make a difference"*. Good. It's a strong word.

JOHN "JOCKO" WILLINK

THE NAVY SEAL STAND

*This is **"The Stand"** that every US Navy SEAL must learn.*

In times of war or uncertainty there is a special breed of warrior ready to answer our Nation's call. A common man with uncommon desire to succeed. Forged by adversity, he stands alongside America's finest special operations forces to serve his country, the American people, and protect their way of life. I am that man. My Trident is a symbol of honour and heritage. Bestowed upon me by the heroes that have gone before, it embodies the trust of those I have sworn to protect. By wearing the Trident I accept the responsibility of my chosen profession and way of life. It is a privilege that I must earn every day. My loyalty to Country and Team is beyond reproach. I humbly serve as a guardian to my fellow Americans always ready to defend those who are unable to defend themselves. I do not advertise the nature of my work, nor seek recognition for my actions. I voluntarily accept the inherent hazards of my profession, placing the welfare and security of others before my own. I serve with honour on and off the battlefield. The ability to control my emotions and my actions, regardless of circumstance, sets me apart from other men. Uncompromising integrity is my standard. My character and honour are steadfast. My word is my bond. We expect to lead and be led. In the absence of orders I will take charge, lead my teammates and accomplish the mission. I lead by example in all situations. I will never quit. I persevere and thrive on adversity. My Nation expects me to be physically harder and mentally stronger than my enemies. If knocked down, I will get back up, every time. I will draw on every remaining ounce of strength to protect my teammates and to accomplish our mission. I am never out of the fight. We demand discipline. We expect innovation. The lives of my teammates and the success of our mission depend on me – my technical skill, tactical proficiency, and attention to detail. My training is never complete. We train for war and fight to win. I stand ready to bring the full spectrum of combat power to bear in order to achieve my mission and the goals established by my country. The execution of my duties will be swift and violent when required yet guided by the very principles that I serve to defend. Brave men have fought and died building the proud tradition and feared reputation that I am bound to uphold. In the worst of conditions, the legacy of my teammates steadies my resolve and silently guides my every deed.

I will not fail.

#**TEN**WORDS

OPRAH WINFREY

"Surround yourself with people who will only lift you higher".

Oprah is a truly remarkable media phenomenon and only one of a handful of people in the world who are recognised simply by their first name. From humble beginnings within a poor and unstable family, she has emerged as one of the most influential people on the planet. Oprah has always been a great storyteller, a skill she learned from her father and a talent that landed Oprah her first job at a local radio station when she was still in high school. After graduating college in 1976 (*with a degree in speech and communication*), she accepted her dream job as a reporter with WTVF-TV and by the time she was 19, she became the first black female anchor on the nightly news in her home town of Nashville.

"You can have it all – just not all at once".

Oprah continued to develop her communication skills as the host of a daytime talk show called *"People are Talking"*, but it wasn't until 1984 when she moved to Chicago to work on a morning chat show that she became famous. The show, originally called AM Chicago, was expanded to an hour and renamed The Oprah Winfrey Show and syndicated to a national audience the following year. The rest, as they say, is history. She is now recognised all over the world not only as a media tycoon, entrepreneur, actress and philanthropist, but as one of the best storytellers on our screens.

Oprah has been voted by TIME magazine as one of the 100 most influential people of the 20th century with a person net worth of over $3Bn. In 2004 I wrote about her in my book, *Sex, Brands and Rock'n'Roll* when she was honored by the United Nations with a Global Humanitarian Award after donating $40M to found the Oprah Winfrey Leadership Academy for Girls in Johannesburg.

READ: O! Magazine
WATCH: *OWN* (Oprah Winfrey TV Network)
FOLLOW: @OprahWinfrey

#**TEN**WORDS

OPRAH WINFREY

"One of life's greatest risks is never daring to risk„.

#**TEN**WORDS

ANNA WINTOUR

"Why fit in when you were born to stand out?"

With an estimated salary of $2 million and a staff uniform budget of around $200,000), Vogue's Editor-in-Chief Anna Wintour certainly leads the kind of lifestyle any fashionista would envy, but it is her substance, not just her style, which makes her unique.

READ: Vogue
WATCH: *The September Issue* by R.J. Cutler
FOLLOW: @Vogue

There is no one in the fashion world quite as powerful or as polarising as Anna Wintour, the American Vogue editor-in-chief. She is currently leading Vogue through its 125th anniversary amidst a political, economic and technological disruption that is shaking the very foundations of the global fashion industry over which she has ruled like a head of state for almost 30 years. Donning her trademark black Chanel sunglasses and perfectly styled bob, Wintour has been a fashion-show fixture for decades.

I have followed and admired her career from a distance, but like most people who don't know her, I have been always been slightly bemused by her icy *Devil-Wears-Prada-esque* persona, her lack of visible emotions and her ever present shades. All leading fashion designers have cultivated a unique image over the course of their career, but for Anna - her image is more than that. It is her protective clothing, helping her to cope with the challenges that her role gives her. As for her signature look, Wintour has reportedly sported a bob since she was 15 years old. The black Chanel sunglasses serve a purpose beyond fashion. She told 60 Minutes in 2009, "*I can sit in a show and if I am bored out of my mind, nobody will notice ... At this point, they have become, really, armour.*" Every one should find an image that works for them and stick with it. Because why would you ever want to fit in, when you were born to stand out?

#**TEN**WORDS

ANNA WINTOUR

"It's not what you make, it's what you stand for".

#TENWORDS

Sir TERRY WOGAN

"My opinion has the weight of a ton of feathers".

All of the best presenters I've ever seen or had the pleasure of working with all agree on one thing, it is never about them, it's about the audience. Being able to consistently win over an audience with self-deprecating humour, clever comments and quick wits is no easy task, so when you get recognised by a broadcaster and paid millions to be the face of their organisation, you can be forgiven for having a bit of an ego. Sir Terry Wogan had no ego whatsoever and very little desire to force his opinions on others. I always thought he was the ultimate presenter. Sir Terry worked for the BBC for 50 years, and despite receiving all the honours and awards that a top class presenter could hope to win, Terry's audiences adored him most because he always wanted the spotlight to be on someone else. Especially people who *really* needed it. So instead of constantly hogging the spotlight, Sir Terry chose to dedicate his life to the BBC's Children in Need, raising over £800 million for disadvantaged young people as the figurehead of the charity.

Not long before he died, Sir Terry was asked what his golden rule of presenting was. Without a moments hesitation he repeated his *"ten words"* suggesting that his opinion wasn't all that valuable, and then in true Wogan style, with a twinkle in his eye, he said, *"Get on your toes, keep your wits about you, say goodnight politely when it's over, go home and enjoy your dinner"*. Legend.

One of the reasons Sir Terry was so successful as a presenter (especially on radio) was because he understood his position but insisted on making the most of it, *"We're not talking to an audience. You're talking to one person and they're only half-listening. It's a mistake to think that everybody's clinging to your every word"*.

READ: *Is it Me?* By Terry Wogan
WATCH: Children in Need: Tribute to Sir Terry
FOLLOW: @BBCCiN

#**TEN**WORDS

ZIG ZIGLAR

"The right quote can inspire people to change their ways".

When I got my first real job as a salesman in a hi-fi store, I bought a copy of *Zig Ziglar's Guide to Selling* from my local Waterstone's store in Manchester. I still have it. Most of the margins have notes written in them, many of the pages are folded over, and there are countless drinks stains on the cover from the bars that I took it to when I was first reading it. I wanted to learn everything that Zig said. Not just because he was widely regarded as America's greatest sales trainer, but because his words seemed to have substance to them. There was one quote in particular which I'll never forget. It's a quote which I still use today and is the best piece of advice I've ever received. I write it on the opening page of every new notebook I buy.

"You can get everything in life you want if you will just help enough other people get what they want".

Over the course of his life, Zig helped a lot of people to get what they want. He is certainly the best motivational speaker I have ever heard, because his quotes have so much depth. Over twenty years later I can still remember quotes I read in his books or heard on his cassette seminars! I remember them because he never just threw out bumper sticker advice, he made sure that you understood exactly what you needed to do to become better. Seth Godin calls him the greatest marketer ever. I totally agree.

During his career Zig travelled over 5 million miles giving seminars to business people keen to improve their sales skills and self-image. For over 40 years he was America's top motivational speaker, writing 30 books, but he says his greatest achievement was being married to *"the redhead"* for 65 years.

READ: *See You At The Top* by Zig Ziglar
WATCH: Any of Zig's seminars on YouTube
FOLLOW: @TheZigZiglar

#TENWORDS

MARK ZUCKERBERG

"Our mission is to connect every person in the world".

"A squirrel dying in front of your house may be more relevant to your interests right now than people dying in Africa".

Zuckerberg wants to change the world through initiatives such as Internet.org, but he also understands that in order to do that, social networks are usually built upon the less pressing concerns which are most relevant to their users.

READ: The Facebook Effect by David Kirkpatrick
WATCH: The Social Network by David Fincher
FOLLOW: Facebook.com/Mark

When Mark Zuckerberg began to build the world's largest social network, his ten world mission statement was to make the world more open and connected. You don't embark upon a mission like that with any short term goals. Mark Zuckerberg has a long term view. And by long, I mean LONG. I once heard a conversation where Andrew Bosworth, (*Facebook's Head of Product Development*), mentioned that one of the reasons Facebook is so successful is because Zuckerberg had a *"geological view"*. He was referring to the fact that the Facebook co-founder looks at the world in 100-year cycles, and thinks about the impact that technology will have centuries ahead. Few CEO's including Paul Polman (*Unilever*), Ginni Rometty (*IBM*) and Elon Musk (*Tesla / SpaceX*) have similar geological views. Zuck's geological world view was shaped in school where he loved the classics. His favourite book is Virgil's *Aeneid* and on his college application, Zuck listed French, Hebrew, Latin, and ancient Greek as non-English languages he could read and write.

The marketing industry does not pride itself on having a long-term view. Campaigns are run over short periods and ROI is calculated from immediate gains. I commissioned some research in 2016 of 1,200 marketers to see how much short-term thinking existed in the marketing industry and was staggered to discover that two-thirds of marketers did not have a long-term view of their customers.

#**TEN**WORDS

MARK ZUCKERBERG

It's easy to be sceptical and argue that despite his education, someone like Zuckerberg only cares about selling more ads and making money, but in my opinion, that's simply not true. Of course, it's easy to say that now because he's allegedly worth over $50Bn, but in the early days of Facebook when he was still a student hitting his friends up for small business loans, he could easily have made bad decisions if financial gain has his primary motivation. This is all anecdotal of course, but consider some of the deals he turned down in those first few years...

Companies that tried (and failed) to buy Facebook:

- **Anonymous**: $10m (July 2004)
- **Friendster**: undisclosed
- **Google**: speculative
- **Viacom**: $75m (March 2005)
- **MySpace**: undisclosed (Spring 2005)
- **Viacom**: undisclosed (Fall 2005)
- **News Corp**: undisclosed (Jan 2006)
- **Viacom**: $1.5Bn (Early 2006)
- **AOL**: $1Bn+ (2006)
- **Yahoo**: $1Bn+ (Fall 2006)
- **Google**: Undisclosed (2007)
- **Microsoft**: $15Bn (2007)

The most telling piece of evidence about Zuckerberg's 'geological view' to me was the fact that he turned down $10m from an anonymous New York financier when Facebook was only 5 months old, while he was still a student. That's not the actions of a guy who is only driven by financial gain. Cliches aside, Zuckerberg really does want to make the world a *better place*. And judging by the pledges he has made with his wife through their *Chan Zuckerberg Initiative*, 99% of their wealth (approx $50Bn) is being donated to philanthropic causes to help fight diseases. For a hacker who initially built THE social network in order to meet girls, that's not a bad legacy to leave behind.

MOVE FAST AND BREAK THINGS

These were the 140 gorgeous people* who inspired me in just Ten Words.

Collecting their quotes and curating their words has been a joy. I hope you enjoyed reading it as much as I enjoyed writing it. If so, please tweet nice things using #TenWords

* I was keen to make **Ten Words** *"personal"* and not make it just another random list of interesting (or "influential") people, so I have chosen to only write about people who I have either met, keynoted with or spoken about in my presentations. I also resisted the temptation to organise each person using any kind of rankings because most rankings are dumb and entirely subjective. Thanks for reading. Tell your friends! x

#TENWORDS

Thank You.

Many people made this book possible. This is a book about the people who have inspired me in business, but none of this would have been possible without the support of my friends and colleagues. I'm not the easiest person to work or live with as my head is usually in the clouds or racing off in one hundred different directions! Writing a book is a very indulgent and time-consuming process, especially when you are writing it as much for yourself as you are for an audience, so I must first give thanks to my wife Ginger for giving me the time and space to write it while she looked after our twins Petra and Mathilda. My son Lewis Waite who is a genuine rock star and will no doubt end up featuring in a book like this some day himself. My mum and dad for dropping me onto this planet in the first place. Much love also to my employers (past and present) Adobe, Salesforce and IBM for giving me the opportunity to meet so many of the wonderful people who appear in this book and for forgiving my many shortcomings as one of the worst people at doing admin or replying quickly to emails. Julia Jackson for helping to inspire this whole thing in the first place with our "one hundred days" chat and especially Sarah Parsonage who carried out the epic task of helping to edit my schizophrenic writing style and late night ramblings.

A *huge* thank you to all my friends, colleagues and the many business leaders who continue to inspire me every day by trying to change things. There are many (and I will forget some for which I will apologise in advance and make it up to you with cocktails when we meet) but they include:

William Adams, Ajaz Ahmed, Chris Anderson, Paul Arden, Neil Argent, Juliet Avery, Andy Barr, Marc Benioff, Russell Braterman, Scott Brinker, Chris Brogan, Melanie Butcher, Fiona Byrd, Matt Candy, Jack Canfield, Emily Chang, Margaret Carter, Vikki Chowney, Clay Christensen, Dave Coplin, Brian Cox, Chris Dacre, Minter Dial, Mark Dickson, Ally Dowsing-Reynolds, Adam Dyer, Drew Ellis, Dave Farrow, Tim Ferris, Tom Fishburne, Fletch Fletcher, Tom Ford, Carmine Gallo, Scott Galloway, Lisa Gilbert, Seth Godin, Ed Goodman, Harriet Green, Andrew Grill, Jeff Hammerbacher, Parker Harris, Andy Hawthorne, Richard Hearn, Brian Houston, Charlie Hugh-Jones, Jon Iwata, Mark Jackson, Zachary Jeans, Mitch Joel, Travis Kalanick, Avinash Kaushik, Guy Kawasaki, John Kelly, Kevin Kelly, David Kerr, Chip Kidd, Austin Kleon, Gabrielle Laine-Peters, Javier Sanchez-Lamalas, Natalie Lamb, Michael Lazerow, Fiona Lugton, Hugh Macleod, Judd Marcello, John C. Maxwell, Neeta McAndrew, Jon Mell, Jason Miller, Lauren Mort, Ruth Mortimer, Nick Noble, Dara O'Briain, Freddie Ossberg, Dave Parkinson, Russell Parsons, Michelle Pelluso, Tom Peters, Eugene Peterson, David JP Phillips, Hugo Pinto, Micah Purnell, David Raab, Mark Ritson, Tony Robbins, Rebecca Robbins, David Robinson, Ted Rubin, Richard Rumelt, Ginni Rometty, Peter Saville, Paul Scanlon, Ken Segall, Jason Silva, Mark Simpson, Simon Sinek, Tom Smith, Paul Smith, Brian Solis, Aaron Sorkin, Biz Stone, Caleb Storkey, Scott Stratton, Rory Sutherland, Caroline Taylor, Emma Taylor, John Trowell, Gary Vaynerchuk, James and Sarah Walker, John Watton, Linz West, James Whatley, Jenny Whitham, Maria Winans, Neil Woodcock, Kareem Yusuf.

People will always sum up your life in one sentence...

What's yours?